SCOTT FORESMAN

Reading Street
COMMON CORE

P9-CCI-134

Reading Street
Common Core
Writing
to Sources

Glenview, Illinois

Boston, Massachusetts

Chandler, Arizona

Upper Saddle River, New Jersey

ALWAYS LEARNING   PEARSON

ISBN-13: 978-0-328-76858-5
ISBN-10: 0-328-76858-8
6 7 8 9 10 V0N4 15 14

Reading Street Common Core
Writing to Sources

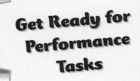

Get Ready for Performance Tasks

Reading Street Common Core Writing to Sources makes fact-finding fun! Students substantiate their claims and communicate in writing what they have learned from one text and then from other related texts.

Reading Street Common Core Writing to Sources encourages students to collaborate and share their growing knowledge with peers, adding quality experiences in the art of using text-based evidence.

Reading Street Common Core Writing to Sources provides more practice with all modes of writing—argument, informative/explanatory, and narrative—and connects to the Common Core State Standards.

Reading Street Common Core Writing to Sources gives students opportunities to complete Performance Tasks by writing in response to what they read and collaborating with others.

Reading Street Common Core Writing to Sources offers you an alternative approach to writing tasks on Reading Street!

1 Write Like a Reporter
   Write to one source.
   Students respond to the main selection by citing evidence from the text.

2 Connect the Texts
   Write to two sources.
   Students respond to the main and paired selections by citing evidence from the texts.

3 Prove It! Unit Writing Task
   Write to multiple sources.
   Students analyze multiple sources within a unit and cite evidence from the texts.

4 More Connect the Texts
   Additional lessons specific to writing forms within all modes of writing—argument, informative/explanatory, and narrative—are included.

"Write Like a Reporter!"

Table of Contents

Get Ready for Performance Tasks

Unit 1 Turning Points

Writing Focus: Narrative

Write Like a Reporter
Narrative Paragraph

> **Student Prompt** Reread the story on pp. 32–36 that Miss Franny tells Opal about her encounter with the bear. Create a list of the main events of the bear encounter in order. Then write a one-paragraph narrative that retells the events about Miss Franny and the bear from a different character's perspective. Use third-person point of view and include transitions, such as *first, next,* and *then,* to show the sequence of events. Also include dialogue, description, and sensory details based on the original text.

_____

_____

_____

_____

_____

_____

_____

_____

_____

_____

_____

_____

_____

Write Like a Reporter
Narrative Paragraph

> **Student Prompt, p. 6** Reread the story on pp. 32–36 that Miss Franny tells Opal about her encounter with the bear. Create a list of the main events of the bear encounter in order. Then write a one-paragraph narrative that retells the events about Miss Franny and the bear from a different character's perspective. Use third-person point of view and include transitions, such as *first, next,* and *then,* to show the sequence of events. Also include dialogue, description, and sensory details based on the original text.

Writing to Sources After students reread the passage, have them list the events in order. Point out that the original story is told in first person, from Miss Franny's perspective. Remind students to write their narratives from a *different* character's perspective, in third person (using *she* instead of *I*). In their narratives, students should introduce the main characters (Miss Franny and the bear) and retell the main events in order, using transitions to make the order clear. They should also include dialogue and sensory details to develop the scene. Remind students to reread the text carefully and base their narratives on details from the story.

Students' paragraphs should:
- orient the reader by introducing the narrator and characters
- use dialogue to show the responses of characters to situations
- use transitional words and phrases to show sequence of events
- demonstrate strong command of the conventions of standard written English

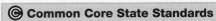 **Common Core State Standards**

Writing 3. Write narratives to develop real or imagined experiences or events using effective technique, descriptive details, and clear event sequences. **Writing 9.** Draw evidence from literary or informational texts to support analysis, reflection, and research. **Writing 9.a.** Apply grade 4 Reading standards to literature (e.g., "Describe in depth a character, setting, or event in a story or drama, drawing on specific details in the text [e.g., a character's thoughts, words, or actions].").

Connect the Texts
Narrative Dialogue

Student Prompt Look back at *Because of Winn-Dixie* and "A Film with a Message of Hope." Consider the events of the story and compare them to the main events the movie reviewer describes. Write a two-paragraph dialogue between the author of the story, Kate DiCamillo, and the movie reviewer, Robert Sparks, about specific details mentioned in the story that are not mentioned in the review. Use main events, details, and descriptions from both passages as you write the dialogue.

_____

_____

_____

_____

_____

_____

_____

_____

_____

_____

_____

_____

_____

_____

Connect the Texts
Narrative Dialogue

> **Student Prompt, p. 8** Look back at *Because of Winn-Dixie* and "A Film with a Message of Hope." Consider the events of the story and compare them to the main events the movie reviewer describes. Write a two-paragraph dialogue between the author of the story, Kate DiCamillo, and the movie reviewer, Robert Sparks, about specific details mentioned in the story that are not mentioned in the review. Use main events, details, and descriptions from both passages as you write the dialogue.

Writing to Sources Discuss the major parts of the plot of the passage from *Because of Winn-Dixie* that the movie review does not reference. Then have students create a dialogue between the two authors about these events and details. Have students look carefully at both passages and use references from both as they write their dialogues.

		4-point Narrative Writing Rubric			
Score	**Narrative Focus**	**Organization**	**Development of Narrative**	**Language and Vocabulary**	**Conventions**
4	Narrative is clearly focused and developed throughout.	Narrative has a well-developed, logical, easy-to-follow plot.	Narrative includes thorough and effective use of details, dialogue, and description.	Narrative uses precise, concrete sensory language as well as figurative language and/or domain-specific vocabulary.	Narrative has correct grammar, usage, spelling, capitalization, and punctuation.
3	Narrative is mostly focused and developed throughout.	Narrative has a plot, but there may be some lack of clarity and/or unrelated events.	Narrative includes adequate use of details, dialogue and description.	Narrative uses adequate sensory and figurative language and/or domain-specific vocabulary.	Narrative has a few errors but is completely understandable.
2	Narrative is somewhat developed but may occasionally lose focus.	Narrative's plot is difficult to follow, and ideas are not connected well.	Narrative includes only a few details, dialogues, and descriptions.	Language in narrative is not precise or sensory; lacks domain-specific vocabulary.	Narrative has some errors in usage, grammar, spelling and/or punctuation.
1	Narrative may be confusing, unfocused, or too short.	Narrative has little or no apparent plot.	Narrative includes few or no details, dialogue or description.	Language in narrative is vague, unclear, or confusing.	Narrative is hard to follow because of frequent errors.
0	Narrative gets no credit if it does not demonstrate adequate command of narrative writing traits.				

©️ Common Core State Standards

Writing 3. Write narratives to develop real or imagined experiences or events using effective technique, descriptive details, and clear event sequences. **Writing 9.** Draw evidence from literary or informational texts to support analysis, reflection, and research. **Writing 9.a.** Apply grade 4 Reading standards to literature (e.g., "Describe in depth a character, setting, or event in a story or drama, drawing on specific details in the text [e.g., a character's thoughts, words, or actions]."). **Writing 9.b.** Apply grade 4 Reading standards to information texts (e.g., "Explain how an author uses reasons and evidence to support particular points in a text").

Name _____

Write Like a Reporter
Narrative Paragraph

> **Student Prompt** Reread pp. 62–64 where the Native Americans meet Lewis and Seaman, and retell the main events of the story in sequence. Make notes about the details, characters, and setting in this part of the story. Then write a one-paragraph narrative that continues the story from the point of view of the Native Americans. Use transitions, such as *first, next,* and *then,* to show the sequence of events. Develop the characters and include dialogue, description, and sensory details based on details in the original text.

_____

_____

_____

_____

_____

_____

_____

_____

_____

_____

_____

_____

_____

_____

Write Like a Reporter
Narrative Paragraph

> **Student Prompt, p. 10** Reread pp. 62–64 where the Native Americans meet Lewis and Seaman, and retell the main events of the story in sequence. Make notes about the details, characters, and setting in this part of the story. Then write a one-paragraph narrative that continues the story from the point of view of the Native Americans. Use transitions, such as *first, next,* and *then,* to show the sequence of events. Develop the characters and include dialogue, description, and sensory details based on details in the original text.

Writing to Sources After students reread the passage, have them list each event in sequence and list details of the plot, the main characters, and the setting. Remind them to write their narratives from the perspective of the Native Americans. Students should develop the characters and focus on presenting the main events of the story in sequence, using transitions to make the order clear. They should also include dialogue and sensory details to develop the scene. Remind students to reread the text carefully and base their narratives on details from the original story.

Students' paragraphs should:

- orient the reader by introducing the narrator and characters
- use dialogue to develop experiences and events
- use transitional words and phrases to show the sequence of events
- demonstrate strong command of the conventions of standard written English

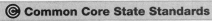 **Common Core State Standards**

Writing 3. Write narratives to develop real or imagined experiences or events using effective technique, descriptive details, and clear event sequences. **Writing 9.** Draw evidence from literary or informational texts to support analysis, reflection, and research. **Writing 9.a.** Apply grade 4 Reading standards to literature (e.g., "Describe in depth a character, setting, or event in a story or drama, drawing on specific details in the text [e.g., a character's thoughts, words, or actions].").

Connect the Texts
Narrative Paragraph

> **Student Prompt** Look back at *Lewis and Clark and Me* and "Ellen Ochoa: Space Pioneer." Make notes that compare and contrast the main ideas, events, characters, and details in the two passages. Consider what Seaman would think if he was aboard a space shuttle instead of a riverboat. Write a one-paragraph narrative from Seaman's point of view as he travels through space. Be sure to include sensory details, characters, and main events based on both readings.

_____

_____

_____

_____

_____

_____

_____

_____

_____

_____

_____

_____

_____

_____

Connect the Texts
Narrative Paragraph

> **Student Prompt, p. 12** Look back at *Lewis and Clark and Me* and "Ellen Ochoa: Space Pioneer." Make notes that compare and contrast the main ideas, events, characters, and details in the two passages. Consider what Seaman would think if he was aboard a space shuttle instead of a riverboat. Write a one-paragraph narrative from Seaman's point of view as he travels through space. Be sure to include sensory details, characters, and main events based on both readings.

Writing to Sources Discuss the main ideas and events of both passages. Students should note sensory details, plot, setting, and characters. Guide them to consider the main ideas, such as exploration or hard work, as they prepare to write narratives about Seaman's experiences in space. The narratives should include sensory details, characters from both passages, and transitions such as *first, then,* and *next* to establish a clear sequence of events.

			4-point Narrative Writing Rubric		
Score	**Narrative Focus**	**Organization**	**Development of Narrative**	**Language and Vocabulary**	**Conventions**
4	Narrative is clearly focused and developed throughout.	Narrative has a well-developed, logical, easy-to-follow plot.	Narrative includes thorough and effective use of details, dialogue, and description.	Narrative uses precise, concrete sensory language as well as figurative language and/or domain-specific vocabulary.	Narrative has correct grammar, usage, spelling, capitalization, and punctuation.
3	Narrative is mostly focused and developed throughout.	Narrative has a plot, but there may be some lack of clarity and/or unrelated events.	Narrative includes adequate use of details, dialogue and description.	Narrative uses adequate sensory and figurative language and/or domain-specific vocabulary.	Narrative has a few errors but is completely understandable.
2	Narrative is somewhat developed but may occasionally lose focus.	Narrative's plot is difficult to follow, and ideas are not connected well.	Narrative includes only a few details, dialogues, and descriptions.	Language in narrative is not precise or sensory; lacks domain-specific vocabulary.	Narrative has some errors in usage, grammar, spelling and/or punctuation.
1	Narrative may be confusing, unfocused, or too short.	Narrative has little or no apparent plot.	Narrative includes few or no details, dialogue or description.	Language in narrative is vague, unclear, or confusing.	Narrative is hard to follow because of frequent errors.
0	Narrative gets no credit if it does not demonstrate adequate command of narrative writing traits.				

© Common Core State Standards

Writing 3. Write narratives to develop real or imagined experiences or events using effective technique, descriptive details, and clear event sequences. **Writing 9.** Draw evidence from literary or informational texts to support analysis, reflection, and research. **Writing 9.a.** Apply grade 4 Reading standards to literature (e.g., "Describe in depth a character, setting, or event in a story or drama, drawing on specific details in the text [e.g., a character's thoughts, words, or actions]."). **Writing 9.b.** Apply grade 4 Reading standards to informational texts (e.g., "Explain how an author uses reasons and evidence to support particular points in a text").

Write Like a Reporter
Narrative Paragraph

Student Prompt Reread the part of the story on pp. 89–92 where Laura and her family visit the swimming hole. List the main events in sequence. Then make notes about the details, characters, and setting in this part of the story. Write a one-paragraph journal entry about the events from Mary's point of view. Use transitions, such as *first, next,* and *then,* to show the sequence of events. Be sure to include sensory details and dialogue between characters.

_____

_____

_____

_____

_____

_____

_____

_____

_____

_____

_____

_____

_____

_____

Write Like a Reporter
Narrative Paragraph

> **Student Prompt, p. 14** Reread the part of the story on pp. 89–92 where Laura and her family visit the swimming hole. List the main events in sequence. Then make notes about the details, characters, and setting in this part of the story. Write a one-paragraph journal entry about the events from Mary's point of view. Use transitions, such as *first, next,* and *then,* to show the sequence of events. Be sure to include sensory details and dialogue between characters.

Writing to Sources After students reread the passage, have them list each event in sequence as well as details of the plot, the main characters, and the setting. Remind them to write their narratives from Mary's perspective. In their narratives, students should develop the characters and present the main events of the story in sequence, using transitions to make the order clear. They should also include dialogue and sensory details to develop the scene and present Mary's point of view. Remind students to reread the text carefully and base their dialogue and descriptions on details from the original story.

Students' paragraphs should:
- orient the reader by establishing a situation
- use dialogue to show the responses of characters to situations
- use sensory details to convey experiences and events precisely
- demonstrate strong command of the conventions of standard written English

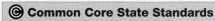
Common Core State Standards

Writing 3. Write narratives to develop real or imagined experiences or events using effective technique, descriptive details, and clear event sequences. **Writing 9.** Draw evidence from literary or informational texts to support analysis, reflection, and research. **Writing 9.a.** Apply grade 4 Reading standards to literature (e.g., "Describe in depth a character, setting, or event in a story or drama, drawing on specific details in the text [e.g., a character's thoughts, words, or actions].").

Name _____

Connect the Texts
Narrative Dialogue

Student Prompt Look back at *On the Banks of Plum Creek* and the online source you found about Laura Ingalls Wilder. Compare and contrast the story and the biographical information you found online. Use your notes about Laura's character, details from the story, and the main events in *On the Banks of Plum Creek* to write a dialogue between the character in the story and the author Laura Ingalls Wilder. Remember to carefully reread both passages as you write your narrative.

_____

_____

_____

_____

_____

_____

_____

_____

_____

_____

_____

_____

_____

_____

Connect the Texts
Narrative Dialogue

Student Prompt, p. 16 Look back at *On the Banks of Plum Creek* and the online source you found about Laura Ingalls Wilder. Compare and contrast the story and the biographical information you found online. Use your notes about Laura's character, details from the story, and the main events in *On the Banks of Plum Creek* to write a dialogue between the character in the story and the author Laura Ingalls Wilder. Remember to carefully reread both passages as you write your narrative.

Writing to Sources Discuss with students the main ideas and events of both passages. Students should make note of sensory details, plot, setting, and characters in the story and of biographical information from the online source. Guide them to consider what the adult Laura would say to the child Laura. Students' dialogues should include sensory details and a clear sequence of events throughout.

		4-point Narrative Writing Rubric			
Score	Narrative Focus	Organization	Development of Narrative	Language and Vocabulary	Conventions
4	Narrative is clearly focused and developed throughout.	Narrative has a well-developed, logical, easy-to-follow plot.	Narrative includes thorough and effective use of details, dialogue, and description.	Narrative uses precise, concrete sensory language as well as figurative language and/or domain-specific vocabulary.	Narrative has correct grammar, usage, spelling, capitalization, and punctuation.
3	Narrative is mostly focused and developed throughout.	Narrative has a plot, but there may be some lack of clarity and/or unrelated events.	Narrative includes adequate use of details, dialogue and description.	Narrative uses adequate sensory and figurative language and/or domain-specific vocabulary.	Narrative has a few errors but is completely understandable.
2	Narrative is somewhat developed but may occasionally lose focus.	Narrative's plot is difficult to follow, and ideas are not connected well.	Narrative includes only a few details, dialogues, and descriptions.	Language in narrative is not precise or sensory; lacks domain-specific vocabulary.	Narrative has some errors in usage, grammar, spelling and/or punctuation.
1	Narrative may be confusing, unfocused, or too short.	Narrative has little or no apparent plot.	Narrative includes few or no details, dialogue or description.	Language in narrative is vague, unclear, or confusing.	Narrative is hard to follow because of frequent errors.
0	Narrative gets no credit if it does not demonstrate adequate command of narrative writing traits.				

© Common Core State Standards

Writing 3. Write narratives to develop real or imagined experiences or events using effective technique, descriptive details, and clear event sequences. **Writing 9.** Draw evidence from literary or informational texts to support analysis, reflection, and research. **Writing 9.a.** Apply grade 4 Reading standards to literature (e.g., "Describe in depth a character, setting, or event in a story or drama, drawing on specific details in the text [e.g., a character's thoughts, words, or actions]."). **Writing 9.b.** Apply grade 4 Reading standards to informational texts (e.g., "Explain how an author uses reasons and evidence to support particular points in a text").

Write Like a Reporter
Narrative Paragraph

Student Prompt Reread and retell pp. 124–129 of the selection, paying close attention to the dialogue between the horned toad and Reba Jo. Then write a two-paragraph newspaper article about the transformation of the horned toad into a charming prince. Interview the main characters, and present the main points of the story. Use transitions, such as *first, next,* and *then,* to show the sequence of events. Be sure to include dialogue, sensory details, and descriptions in your narrative.

_____

_____

_____

_____

_____

_____

_____

_____

_____

_____

_____

_____

_____

_____

Write Like a Reporter
Narrative Paragraph

Student Prompt, p. 18 Reread and retell pp. 124–129 of the selection, paying close attention to the dialogue between the horned toad and Reba Jo. Then write a two-paragraph newspaper article about the transformation of the horned toad into a charming prince. Interview the main characters, and present the main points of the story. Use transitions, such as *first, next,* and *then,* to show the sequence of events. Be sure to include dialogue, sensory details, and descriptions in your narrative.

Writing to Sources After students reread the passage, have them make notes about the main events, characters, plot details, and setting. Remind them to include information from their notes in their newspaper articles. Students should retell the main parts of the story, using transitions such as *first, then,* and *next,* to make the sequence clear. They should also include dialogue and sensory details. Remind them to keep their audience in mind and present the article as if the audience has not already read the story.

Students' paragraphs should:

- orient the reader by establishing a situation
- use dialogue to show the responses of characters to situations
- use transition words and phrases to show sequence of events
- demonstrate strong command of the conventions of standard written English

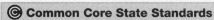
Common Core State Standards

Writing 3. Write narratives to develop real or imagined experiences or events using effective technique, descriptive details, and clear event sequences. **Writing 9.** Draw evidence from literary or informational texts to support analysis, reflection, and research. **Writing 9.a.** Apply grade 4 Reading standards to literature (e.g., "Describe in depth a character, setting, or event in a story or drama, drawing on specific details in the text [e.g., a character's thoughts, words, or actions].").

Connect the Texts
Narrative Dialogue

Student Prompt Carefully reread *The Horned Toad Prince* and "The Fox and the Tiger." Make notes that retell each story. As you make notes, consider what the two genres—trickster tale and fable—have in common. Use your notes to write a dialogue between the horned toad and the fox about their use of trickery and cleverness in each story. Include descriptive language and details from both stories in your narrative.

_____

_____

_____

_____

_____

_____

_____

_____

_____

_____

_____

_____

_____

_____

_____

Connect the Texts
Narrative Dialogue

Student Prompt, p. 20 Carefully reread *The Horned Toad Prince* and "The Fox and the Tiger." Make notes that retell each story. As you make notes, consider what the two genres—trickster tale and fable—have in common. Use your notes to write a dialogue between the horned toad and the fox about their use of trickery and cleverness in each story. Include descriptive language and details from both stories in your narrative.

Writing to Sources Discuss the main characters, events, and genres of both selections. Students should make note of character details, sequences of events, and settings for both stories. Guide them to consider what the horned toad and the fox might have in common and how each character might present his side of the story. Students' dialogues should include descriptive language and clear examples from the selections.

			4-point Narrative Writing Rubric		
Score	**Narrative Focus**	**Organization**	**Development of Narrative**	**Language and Vocabulary**	**Conventions**
4	Narrative is clearly focused and developed throughout.	Narrative has a well-developed, logical, easy-to-follow plot.	Narrative includes thorough and effective use of details, dialogue, and description.	Narrative uses precise, concrete sensory language as well as figurative language and/or domain-specific vocabulary.	Narrative has correct grammar, usage, spelling, capitalization, and punctuation.
3	Narrative is mostly focused and developed throughout.	Narrative has a plot, but there may be some lack of clarity and/or unrelated events.	Narrative includes adequate use of details, dialogue and description.	Narrative uses adequate sensory and figurative language and/or domain-specific vocabulary.	Narrative has a few errors but is completely understandable.
2	Narrative is somewhat developed but may occasionally lose focus.	Narrative's plot is difficult to follow, and ideas are not connected well.	Narrative includes only a few details, dialogues, and descriptions.	Language in narrative is not precise or sensory; lacks domain-specific vocabulary.	Narrative has some errors in usage, grammar, spelling and/or punctuation.
1	Narrative may be confusing, unfocused, or too short.	Narrative has little or no apparent plot.	Narrative includes few or no details, dialogue or description.	Language in narrative is vague, unclear, or confusing.	Narrative is hard to follow because of frequent errors.
0	Narrative gets no credit if it does not demonstrate adequate command of narrative writing traits.				

Ⓒ **Common Core State Standards**

Writing 3. Write narratives to develop real or imagined experiences or events using effective technique, descriptive details, and clear event sequences. **Writing 9.** Draw evidence from literary or informational texts to support analysis, reflection, and research. **Writing 9.a.** Apply grade 4 Reading standards to literature (e.g., "Describe in depth a character, setting, or event in a story or drama, drawing on specific details in the text [e.g., a character's thoughts, words, or actions].").

Write Like a Reporter
Narrative Paragraph

Student Prompt Reread and retell pp. 151–152 of the selection, paying close attention to details about each animal. Then write a dialogue between two animals or birds living in Yosemite based on what you have learned about their behavior and habitat. The narrative should include descriptive details of the animals or birds and should focus on one of the sites the author describes in the text.

_____

_____

_____

_____

_____

_____

_____

_____

_____

_____

_____

_____

_____

_____

Write Like a Reporter
Narrative Paragraph

Student Prompt, p. 22 Reread and retell pp. 151–152 of the selection, paying close attention to details about each animal. Then write a dialogue between two animals or birds living in Yosemite based on what you have learned about their behavior and habitat. The narrative should include descriptive details of the animals or birds and should focus on one of the sites the author describes in the text.

Writing to Sources After students reread the passage, have them make notes about each type of animal or bird and about their favorite part of the park. Guide students to think about what it might be like to be an animal living in Yosemite. Students should write a dialogue between two animals about one of the places described in the text. Remind them to include sensory details or quotations from the text to develop the narrative.

Students' paragraphs should:
- orient the reader by establishing a situation
- use dialogue to show the responses of characters to situations
- use sensory details to convey experiences and events precisely
- demonstrate strong command of the conventions of standard written English

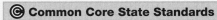 **Common Core State Standards**

Writing 3. Write narratives to develop real or imagined experiences or events using effective technique, descriptive details, and clear event sequences. **Writing 9.** Draw evidence from literary or informational texts to support analysis, reflection, and research. **Writing 9.b.** Apply grade 4 Reading standards to informational texts (e.g., "Explain how an author uses reasons and evidence to support particular points in a text").

Connect the Texts
Narrative Letter

Student Prompt Look back at *Letters Home from Yosemite* and the article "The Bison of Caprock Canyons." Compare the two expository texts, considering what main ideas they have in common. Think about the type of details and descriptions the author uses in *Letters Home from Yosemite* and write a similar letter home from Caprock Canyons. Include descriptive language and details in your narrative. Remember to carefully reread both passages before you write.

_____

_____

_____

_____

_____

_____

_____

_____

_____

_____

_____

_____

_____

Connect the Texts
Narrative Letter

Student Prompt, p. 24 Look back at *Letters Home from Yosemite* and the article "The Bison of Caprock Canyons." Compare the two expository texts, considering what main ideas they have in common. Think about the type of details and descriptions the author uses in *Letters Home from Yosemite* and write a similar letter home from Caprock Canyons. Include descriptive language and details in your narrative. Remember to carefully reread both passages before you write.

Writing to Sources Discuss the purpose and style of both genres of expository writing. Students should make note of the kinds of details, events, and descriptions in *Letters Home from Yosemite*. Guide them to consider how they might use a similar style to write a letter home from Caprock Canyons. Students' narratives should include clear examples from "The Bison of Caprock Canyons" and descriptive language.

		4-point Narrative Writing Rubric			
Score	Narrative Focus	Organization	Development of Narrative	Language and Vocabulary	Conventions
4	Narrative is clearly focused and developed throughout.	Narrative has a well-developed, logical, easy-to-follow plot.	Narrative includes thorough and effective use of details, dialogue, and description.	Narrative uses precise, concrete sensory language as well as figurative language and/or domain-specific vocabulary.	Narrative has correct grammar, usage, spelling, capitalization, and punctuation.
3	Narrative is mostly focused and developed throughout.	Narrative has a plot, but there may be some lack of clarity and/or unrelated events.	Narrative includes adequate use of details, dialogue and description.	Narrative uses adequate sensory and figurative language and/or domain-specific vocabulary.	Narrative has a few errors but is completely understandable.
2	Narrative is somewhat developed but may occasionally lose focus.	Narrative's plot is difficult to follow, and ideas are not connected well.	Narrative includes only a few details, dialogues, and descriptions.	Language in narrative is not precise or sensory; lacks domain-specific vocabulary.	Narrative has some errors in usage, grammar, spelling and/or punctuation.
1	Narrative may be confusing, unfocused, or too short.	Narrative has little or no apparent plot.	Narrative includes few or no details, dialogue or description.	Language in narrative is vague, unclear, or confusing.	Narrative is hard to follow because of frequent errors.
0	Narrative gets no credit if it does not demonstrate adequate command of narrative writing traits.				

Ⓒ Common Core State Standards

Writing 3. Write narratives to develop real or imagined experiences or events using effective technique, descriptive details, and clear event sequences. **Writing 9.** Draw evidence from literary or informational texts to support analysis, reflection, and research. **Writing 9.b.** Apply grade 4 Reading standards to informational texts (e.g., "Explain how an author uses reasons and evidence to support particular points in a text").

Prove It!
Narrative Short Story

New Encounters

Narrative Short Story

In this unit, students have had the opportunity to write in the narrative mode. Remind students of texts and writing tasks (such as Write Like a Reporter and Connect the Texts) in which they have encountered and practiced narrative writing.

Key Features of a Narrative Short Story

- creates a situation and introduces the narrator and characters
- organizes a sequence of events
- uses dialogue and description to develop characters and events
- uses transitions to show sequence
- uses concrete words and sensory details to convey events
- provides a conclusion developed from the events

Writing Task Overview

Each unit writing task provides students with an opportunity to write to sources. To successfully complete the task, students must analyze, synthesize, and evaluate multiple complex texts and create their own written response.

New Encounters

Part 1: Students will reread and take notes on the selected sources. They will then respond to several questions about these sources and discuss their written responses with partners or in small groups.

Part 2: Students will work individually to plan, write, and revise their own narrative short story.

Scorable Products: evidence-based short responses, a short story

New Encounters: Writing Task – Short Response

Teacher Directions:

1. **Introduce the Sources** Refer students to the following texts in the Student Edition:

   1. *Because of Winn-Dixie,* pp. 26–37

   2. *On the Banks of Plum Creek,* pp. 84–99

   3. *The Fox and the Tiger,* pp. 134–135

   Explain to students that they will need to draw evidence and support from the texts above in order to answer evidence-based short response questions and to write a narrative short story. Students should take notes and categorize information as they closely reread the texts. Students should be given paper or a relevant graphic organizer from the TR DVD for note-taking.

2. **Provide Student Directions and Scoring Information (p. 30)** Answer any task-related questions students may have. If necessary, provide additional paper for students to write their responses.

3. **Initiate the Writing Task** If you are timing this part of the task, you may wish to alert students when half the allotted time has elapsed and again when 5 minutes remain.

4. **Facilitate Collaboration** After students have completed their written responses to the evidence-based short response questions, assign partners so that students can discuss their responses. As needed, provide rules and strategies for students to express ideas as well as to link to and build on those of their classmates.

ⓒ Common Core State Standards

Writing 3. Write narratives to develop real or imagined experiences or events using effective technique, descriptive details, and clear event sequences. **Speaking/Listening 1.** Engage effectively in a range of collaborative discussions (one-on-one, in groups, and teacher-led) with diverse partners on grade 4 topics and texts, building on others' ideas and expressing their own clearly.

Scoring Information

Use the following 2-point scoring rubrics to evaluate students' answers to the evidence-based short response questions.

1. Compare and contrast how the authors use description to reveal the characters of Laura, Opal, and the fox. Include evidence from each text as support.

Analysis Rubric	
2	The response: • demonstrates the ability to analyze similarities and differences among characters in the texts • includes specific details that make reference to the texts
1	The response: • demonstrates a limited ability to analyze similarities and differences among characters in the texts • includes some details that make reference to the texts
0	A response receives no credit if it demonstrates no ability to analyze similarities and differences among the texts or includes no relevant details from the texts.

2. Reread the dialogue in each story. What common traits does the dialogue reveal about Laura, Opal, and the fox? Support your answer with key words and phrases from the texts.

Synthesis Rubric	
2	The response: • demonstrates the ability to synthesize information from the sources in order to determine how dialogue reveals character • includes specific details that make reference to the texts
1	The response: • demonstrates a limited ability to synthesize information from the sources in order to determine how dialogue reveals character • includes some details that make reference to the texts
0	A response receives no credit if it demonstrates no ability to synthesize information from the sources or includes no relevant details from the texts.

3. In the three texts, decide whether you learn more about the characters through description or through dialogue. Give details and examples from the texts as support.

	Evaluation Rubric	
2	The response: • demonstrates the ability to evaluate which narrative techniques most effectively reveal character • includes specific details that make reference to the texts	
1	The response: • demonstrates a limited ability to evaluate which narrative techniques most effectively reveal character • includes some details that make reference to the texts	
0	A response receives no credit if it demonstrates no ability to evaluate narrative techniques from the sources or includes no relevant details from the texts.	

© **Common Core State Standards**

Writing 8. Recall relevant information from experiences or gather relevant information from print and digital sources; take notes and categorize information, and provide a list of sources. **Writing 9.** Draw evidence from literary or informational texts to support analysis, reflection, and research.

Name _____

New Encounters
Writing Task – Short Response

Student Directions:

Your assignment You will reread several selections from Unit 1 and take notes on these sources. Then you will answer three questions about these materials. You may refer to your notes or to any of the sources as often as you like.

Sources

1. *Because of Winn-Dixie,* pp. 26–37

2. *On the Banks of Plum Creek,* pp. 84–99

3. *The Fox and the Tiger,* pp. 134–135

Be sure to read closely and take good notes. Your sources and notes will be the basis for writing your own short story in the second half of this writing task.

Evidence-Based Short Response Questions Answer the short response questions on the lines provided below each question. Your answers to these questions will be scored. Be sure to base your answers on the sources you have just read. Remember that you may refer back to your notes or to any of the sources.

After you have answered the questions, you will discuss your responses with a partner or within a small group. Your teacher will let you know when to begin the discussion part of this task.

Scoring Information Your responses will be scored based on how you demonstrate the ability to:

- compare and contrast information from multiple texts
- describe character traits revealed through dialogue
- evaluate description and dialogue
- include specific details that clearly reference the sources

Name_____

Evidence-Based Short Response Questions

1. Compare and contrast how the authors use description to reveal the characters of Laura, Opal, and the fox. Include evidence from each text as support.

_____

_____

_____

_____

2. Reread the dialogue in each story. What common traits does the dialogue reveal about Laura, Opal, and the fox? Support your answer with key words and phrases from the texts.

_____

_____

_____

_____

3. In the three texts, decide whether you learn more about the characters through description or through dialogue. Give details and examples from the texts as support.

_____

_____

_____

_____

Collaborative Discussion

After you have written your responses to the questions, discuss your ideas. Your teacher will assign you a partner or a small group and let you know when to begin.

New Encounters: Writing Task – Short Story

Teacher Directions:

1. Provide Student Directions and Scoring Information (p. 34) Explain to students that they will now review their notes and sources, and plan, draft, and revise their narrative short stories. Although they may use their notes and sources, they must work alone. Students will be allowed to look back at the answers they wrote for the short response questions, but they are not allowed to make changes to those answers. Have students read the directions for the short story. Answer any task-related questions they may have. Students should be given paper on which to write their narrative short stories.

2. Initiate the Writing Task If you are timing this part of the task, you may wish to suggest approximate times for students to begin writing and revising. If students wish to continue writing rather than revising, allow them to do so. Alert students when 5 minutes remain.

3. Scoring Information Use the scoring rubric on the next page to evaluate students' short stories.

4. Short Story Prompt Use what you have learned about the characters in *Because of Winn-Dixie, On the Banks of Plum Creek,* and *The Fox and the Tiger* to write a short story in which two or more characters from different stories meet each other. Include a clear setting and sequence of events, and develop your characters through dialogue and descriptive details. Be sure to follow the conventions of written English.

4-point Narrative Writing Rubric					
Score	Narrative Focus	Organization	Development of Narrative	Language and Vocabulary	Conventions
4	Narrative is clearly focused and developed throughout.	Narrative has a well-developed, logical, easy-to-follow plot.	Narrative includes thorough and effective use of details, dialogue, and description.	Narrative uses precise, concrete sensory language as well as figurative language and/or domain-specific vocabulary.	Narrative has correct grammar, usage, spelling, capitalization, and punctuation.
3	Narrative is mostly focused and developed throughout.	Narrative has a plot, but there may be some lack of clarity and/or unrelated events.	Narrative includes adequate use of details, dialogue and description.	Narrative uses adequate sensory and figurative language and/or domain-specific vocabulary.	Narrative has a few errors but is completely understandable.
2	Narrative is somewhat developed but may occasionally lose focus.	Narrative's plot is difficult to follow, and ideas are not connected well.	Narrative includes only a few details, dialogues, and descriptions.	Language in narrative is not precise or sensory; lacks domain-specific vocabulary.	Narrative has some errors in usage, grammar, spelling and/or punctuation.
1	Narrative may be confusing, unfocused, or too short.	Narrative has little or no apparent plot.	Narrative includes few or no details, dialogue or description.	Language in narrative is vague, unclear, or confusing.	Narrative is hard to follow because of frequent errors.
0	Narrative gets no credit if it does not demonstrate adequate command of narrative writing traits.				

Ⓒ Common Core State Standards

Writing 3. Write narratives to develop real or imagined experiences or events using effective technique, descriptive details, and clear event sequences. **Writing 9.** Draw evidence from literary or informational texts to support analysis, reflection, and research. **(Also Writing 3.a., Writing 3.b., Writing 10.)**

New Encounters
Writing Task – Short Story

Student Directions:

Your assignment Now you will review your notes and sources, and plan, draft, and revise your narrative short story. While you may use your notes and refer to the sources, you must work on your own. You may also refer to the answers you wrote to earlier questions, but you cannot change those answers.

Short Story Prompt Use what you have learned about the characters in *Because of Winn-Dixie, On the Banks of Plum Creek,* and *The Fox and the Tiger* to write a short story in which two or more characters from different stories meet each other. Include a clear setting and sequence of events, and develop your characters through dialogue and descriptive details. Be sure to follow the conventions of written English.

Scoring Information Your short story will be assigned a score for

1. **Focus** – how well you create a situation and introduce the narrator and characters

2. **Organization** – how well you structure a natural order of events, using transitions to show sequence

3. **Elaboration** – how well you use descriptive details and dialogue to develop characters and events

4. **Language and Vocabulary** – how well you describe characters and events using concrete words and sensory language

5. **Conventions** – how well you follow the rules of usage, punctuation, capitalization, and spelling

Now begin work on your narrative short story. Try to manage your time carefully so that you can

- plan your narrative short story
- write your narrative short story
- revise and edit for a final draft

New Encounters: Writing Task – Short Story

Teacher Directions:

1. Publish Explain to students that publishing their writing is the last step in the writing process. If time permits, have students review one another's short stories and incorporate any comments their classmates have. Offer students suggestions for how to use technology to publish their work, such as in a school print anthology, online collection, or blog post. Encourage students to use the Internet to share their work with others.

2. Present Students will now have the option to present their short stories. Have students give readings of their short stories to the class. Use the list below to offer students some tips on listening and speaking.

While Listening to a Classmate...
- Face the speaker to listen attentively.
- Pay close attention to dialogue so you know which character is speaking.

While Speaking to Classmates...
- Determine your purpose for speaking.
- Have good posture and eye contact.
- Speak at an appropriate pace.
- Adapt your voice to fit the characters when reading dialogue.

Things to Do Together...
- Ask and answer questions with detail.
- Clarify or follow up on details presented.
- Contribute to the discussion and expand on each other's ideas.

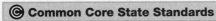 **Common Core State Standards**

Writing 6. With some guidance and support from adults, use technology, including the Internet, to produce and publish writing as well as to interact and collaborate with others; demonstrate sufficient command of keyboarding skills to type a minimum of one page in a single sitting. **Speaking/Listening 1.c.** Pose and respond to specific questions to clarify or follow up on information, and make comments that contribute to the discussion and link to the remarks of others. **Speaking/Listening 4.** Report on a topic or text, tell a story, or recount an experience in an organized manner, using appropriate facts and relevant, descriptive details to support main ideas or themes; speak clearly at an understandable pace.

Unit 2 Teamwork

Writing Focus: Argument

Write Like a Reporter
Argumentative Paragraph

> **Student Prompt** Reread the story *What Jo Did* paying close attention to the sequence of events, the facts, and details. Should Jo have taken off her hat at the beginning of the basketball game? In a one-paragraph argument, tell whether you agree or disagree with Jo's decision. Use evidence from the story to state your opinion and support your argument. Use linking phrases such as *for instance, in order to,* and *in addition* to make your reasoning clear.

_____

_____

_____

_____

_____

_____

_____

_____

_____

_____

_____

_____

Write Like a Reporter

Argumentative Paragraph

Student Prompt, p. 38 Reread the story *What Jo Did* paying close attention to the sequence of events, the facts, and details. Should Jo have taken off her hat at the beginning of the basketball game? In a one-paragraph argument, tell whether you agree or disagree with Jo's decision. Use evidence from the story to state your opinion and support your argument. Use linking phrases such as *for instance, in order to,* and *in addition* to make your reasoning clear.

Writing to Sources After students reread the story, discuss whether Jo should or should not have taken off her hat at the beginning of the basketball game. As students begin their arguments, remind them to state an opinion. Guide them to use facts and details from the story to support their reasoning. Remind students to use linking phrases to make their arguments clear.

Students' paragraphs should:

- state an opinion
- provide reasons that are supported by facts and details from the story
- link opinion and reasons using words and phrases related to the opinion presented
- demonstrate strong command of the conventions of standard written English

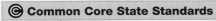 **Common Core State Standards**

Writing 1. Write opinion pieces on topics or texts, supporting a point of view with reasons and information. **Writing 9.** Draw evidence from literary or informational texts to support analysis, reflection, and research. **Writing 9.a.** Apply grade 4 Reading standards to literature (e.g., "Describe in depth a character, setting, or event in a story or drama, drawing on specific details in the text [e.g., a character's thoughts, words, or actions].").

Connect the Texts
Argumentative Essay

> **Student Prompt** Look back at *What Jo Did* and the advertisement "Stickfast Hoop." Consider the main ideas the two readings have in common. Would Jo buy a Stickfast Hoop? Write a one-paragraph argument using details and facts from both texts to support your reasoning. Group your ideas in an organizational structure that clarifies your opinion and support.

_____

_____

_____

_____

_____

_____

_____

_____

_____

_____

_____

_____

_____

_____

_____

_____

Connect the Texts
Argumentative Essay

> **Student Prompt, p. 40** Look back at *What Jo Did* and the advertisement "Stickfast Hoop." Consider the main ideas the two readings have in common. Would Jo buy a Stickfast Hoop? Write a one-paragraph argument using details and facts from both texts to support your reasoning. Group your ideas in an organizational structure that clarifies your opinion and support.

Writing to Sources Discuss the details, facts, and characters in *What Jo Did*. Then discuss the persuasive purpose of the advertisement for the Stickfast Hoop. Guide students to consider how what they know about Jo's character helps them determine whether or not she would want to buy a Stickfast Hoop. Students' arguments should use relevant facts and details from both texts in an organizational structure that makes their reasoning clear.

4-point Argument Writing Rubric				
Score	**Statement of Purpose/Focus**	**Organization**	**Development of Evidence**	**Language and Vocabulary**	**Conventions**
4	Opinion is clearly conveyed and well supported; response is focused.	Organization is clear and effective, creating a sense of cohesion.	Evidence is thorough and persuasive, and includes facts and details.	Ideas are clearly and effectively conveyed, using precise language and/or domain-specific vocabulary.	Command of conventions is strongly demonstrated.
3	Opinion is clear, adequately supported; response is generally focused.	Organization is clear, though minor flaws may be present and some ideas may be disconnected.	Evidence is adequate and includes facts and details.	Ideas are adequately conveyed, using both precise and more general language; may include domain-specific vocabulary.	Command of conventions is sufficiently demonstrated.
2	Opinion is somewhat supported; response may lack focus or include unnecessary material.	Organization is inconsistent, and flaws are apparent.	Evidence is uneven or incomplete; insufficient use of facts and details.	Ideas are unevenly conveyed, using overly-simplistic language; lack of domain-specific vocabulary.	Command of conventions is uneven.
1	The response may be confusing, unfocused; opinion not sufficiently supported.	Organization is poor or nonexistent.	Evidence is poor or nonexistent.	Ideas are conveyed in a vague, unclear, or confusing manner.	There is very little command of conventions.
0	The response shows no evidence of the ability to construct a coherent opinion essay using information from sources.				

ⓒ **Common Core State Standards**

Writing 1. Write opinion pieces on topics or texts, supporting a point of view with reasons and information. **Writing 9.** Draw evidence from literary or informational texts to support analysis, reflection, and research. **Writing 9.a.** Apply grade 4 Reading standards to literature (e.g., "Describe in depth a character, setting, or event in a story or drama, drawing on specific details in the text [e.g., a character's thoughts, words, or actions].").

Name _____

Write Like a Reporter
Argumentative Paragraph

Student Prompt Reread *Coyote School News,* and then focus on the stories in the newspaper. Why are Monchi's stories good? In one paragraph, state your opinion and use details from the reading—including the newspaper—to support your argument. Use linking phrases such as *for instance* and *in addition* to make your reasoning clear.

_____

_____

_____

_____

_____

_____

_____

_____

_____

_____

_____

_____

_____

_____

_____

_____

Write Like a Reporter
Argumentative Paragraph

Student Prompt, p. 42 Reread *Coyote School News,* and then focus on the stories in the newspaper. Why are Monchi's stories good? In one paragraph, state your opinion and use details from the reading—including the newspaper—to support your argument. Use linking phrases such as *for instance* and *in addition* to make your reasoning clear.

Writing to Sources After students reread *Coyote School News,* discuss the stories in the newspaper. Ask students whether Monchi's stories are interesting, clear, and correctly written. Then ask, "Are the stories good?" Students should state an opinion and support it with details from the text. Remind students to use linking words and phrases to make their arguments clear.

Students' paragraphs should:

- clearly state an opinion
- provide reasons that are supported by details from the text
- link opinion and reasons using words and phrases related to the opinion presented
- demonstrate strong command of the conventions of standard written English

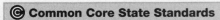 **Common Core State Standards**

Writing 1. Write opinion pieces on topics or texts, supporting a point of view with reasons and information. **Writing 9.** Draw evidence from literary or informational texts to support analysis, reflection, and research. **Writing 9.a.** Apply grade 4 Reading standards to literature (e.g., "Describe in depth a character, setting, or event in a story or drama, drawing on specific details in the text [e.g., a character's thoughts, words, or actions].").

Connect the Texts
Argumentative Essay

Student Prompt Reread *Coyote School News* and "How to Start a School Newspaper." Based on your readings, what kind of editor would help the *Coyote News* school newspaper the most? Write a one-paragraph argumentative essay in which you give your opinion and support it with reasons. Most importantly, support your reasons with details from both readings. Conclude your paragraph with a sentence that relates your reasons and your opinion.

_____

_____

_____

_____

_____

_____

_____

_____

_____

_____

_____

_____

_____

Connect the Texts
Argumentative Essay

Student Prompt, p. 44 Reread *Coyote School News* and "How to Start a School Newspaper." Based on your readings, what kind of editor would help the *Coyote News* school newspaper the most? Write a one-paragraph argumentative essay in which you give your opinion and support it with reasons. Most importantly, support your reasons with details from both readings. Conclude your paragraph with a sentence that relates your reasons and your opinion.

Writing to Sources After students reread the story and the how-to article, have them discuss which kind of editor would benefit the newspaper the most. Then have each student write a one-paragraph argumentative essay in which they use details, such as quotations and facts, from both texts to support their opinions. Have students write a concluding sentence that relates their reasons and their opinion.

	4-point Argument Writing Rubric				
Score	Statement of Purpose/Focus	Organization	Development of Evidence	Language and Vocabulary	Conventions
4	Opinion is clearly conveyed and well supported; response is focused.	Organization is clear and effective, creating a sense of cohesion.	Evidence is thorough and persuasive, and includes facts and details.	Ideas are clearly and effectively conveyed, using precise language and/or domain-specific vocabulary.	Command of conventions is strongly demonstrated.
3	Opinion is clear, adequately supported; response is generally focused.	Organization is clear, though minor flaws may be present and some ideas may be disconnected.	Evidence is adequate and includes facts and details.	Ideas are adequately conveyed, using both precise and more general language; may include domain-specific vocabulary.	Command of conventions is sufficiently demonstrated.
2	Opinion is somewhat supported; response may lack focus or include unnecessary material.	Organization is inconsistent, and flaws are apparent.	Evidence is uneven or incomplete; insufficient use of facts and details.	Ideas are unevenly conveyed, using overly-simplistic language; lack of domain-specific vocabulary.	Command of conventions is uneven.
1	The response may be confusing, unfocused; opinion not sufficiently supported.	Organization is poor or nonexistent.	Evidence is poor or nonexistent.	Ideas are conveyed in a vague, unclear, or confusing manner.	There is very little command of conventions.
0	The response shows no evidence of the ability to construct a coherent opinion essay using information from sources.				

Ⓒ Common Core State Standards

Writing 1. Write opinion pieces on topics or texts, supporting a point of view with reasons and information. **Writing 9.** Draw evidence from literary or informational texts to support analysis, reflection, and research. **Writing 9.a.** Apply grade 4 Reading standards to literature (e.g., "Describe in depth a character, setting, or event in a story or drama, drawing on specific details in the text [e.g., a character's thoughts, words, or actions]."). **Writing 9.b.** Apply grade 4 Reading standards to informational texts (e.g., "Explain how an author uses reasons and evidence to support particular points in a text").

Write Like a Reporter
Argumentative Paragraph

Student Prompt As you reread *Scene Two,* list the sequence of events.
Do you think the characters learned how to solve problems as a team? In a
one-paragraph argument, create an organizational structure that gives your
point of view. Support your opinion with reasons based on details from the
text. Use words or phrases such as *because, for instance, in order to,* and *in
addition* to make your reasoning clear.

_____

_____

_____

_____

_____

_____

_____

_____

_____

_____

_____

_____

_____

_____

_____

Write Like a Reporter
Argumentative Paragraph

> **Student Prompt, p. 46** As you reread *Scene Two*, list the sequence of events. Do you think the characters learned how to solve problems as a team? In a one-paragraph argument, create an organizational structure that gives your point of view. Support your opinion with reasons based on details from the text. Use words or phrases such as *because, for instance, in order to,* and *in addition* to make your reasoning clear.

Writing to Sources After students reread the play, have them list the main events. Students should examine the text for evidence of the characters working as a team and base their opinions on details from the text. Remind students to establish an effective organizational structure and to use linking words and phrases to make sure their arguments are organized and clear.

Students' paragraphs should:

- create an organizational structure in which related ideas are grouped to support the writer's purpose
- provide reasons that are supported by details from the text
- link opinion and reasons using words and phrases related to the opinion presented
- demonstrate strong command of the conventions of standard written English

---

Ⓒ **Common Core State Standards**

Writing 1. Write opinion pieces on topics or texts, supporting a point of view with reasons and information. **Writing 9.** Draw evidence from literary or informational texts to support analysis, reflection, and research. **Writing 9.a.** Apply grade 4 Reading standards to literature (e.g., "Describe in depth a character, setting, or event in a story or drama, drawing on specific details in the text [e.g., a character's thoughts, words, or actions].").

Connect the Texts
Argumentative Essay

Student Prompt Reread *Scene Two* and the poems "Home" and "Front Porch." Compare and contrast how the speakers or characters describe their homes or hometown. Which reading describes the setting and details of the homes or hometown best? State your opinion in an argumentative essay and use details, including quotations, from all three readings to support your opinion. Use linking words and phrases to make your reasoning clear.

_____

_____

_____

_____

_____

_____

_____

_____

_____

_____

_____

_____

_____

_____

_____

_____

Connect the Texts
Argumentative Essay

Student Prompt, p. 48 Reread *Scene Two* and the poems "Home" and "Front Porch." Compare and contrast how the speakers or characters describe their homes or hometown. Which reading describes the setting and details of the homes or hometown best? State your opinion in an argumentative essay and use details, including quotations, from all three readings to support your opinion. Use linking words and phrases to make your reasoning clear.

Writing to Sources After students reread the play and the poems, have them point out descriptive details in the passages. Ask them to write argumentative essays about which passage best describes a home or hometown. Students should include quotations as evidence from each text to support their opinions. Remind students to use linking words and phrases to make their arguments clear.

	4-point Argument Writing Rubric				
Score	**Statement of Purpose/Focus**	**Organization**	**Development of Evidence**	**Language and Vocabulary**	**Conventions**
4	Opinion is clearly conveyed and well supported; response is focused.	Organization is clear and effective, creating a sense of cohesion.	Evidence is thorough and persuasive, and includes facts and details.	Ideas are clearly and effectively conveyed, using precise language and/or domain-specific vocabulary.	Command of conventions is strongly demonstrated.
3	Opinion is clear, adequately supported; response is generally focused.	Organization is clear, though minor flaws may be present and some ideas may be disconnected.	Evidence is adequate and includes facts and details.	Ideas are adequately conveyed, using both precise and more general language; may include domain-specific vocabulary.	Command of conventions is sufficiently demonstrated.
2	Opinion is somewhat supported; response may lack focus or include unnecessary material.	Organization is inconsistent, and flaws are apparent.	Evidence is uneven or incomplete; insufficient use of facts and details.	Ideas are unevenly conveyed, using overly-simplistic language; lack of domain-specific vocabulary.	Command of conventions is uneven.
1	The response may be confusing, unfocused; opinion not sufficiently supported.	Organization is poor or nonexistent.	Evidence is poor or nonexistent.	Ideas are conveyed in a vague, unclear, or confusing manner.	There is very little command of conventions.
0	The response shows no evidence of the ability to construct a coherent opinion essay using information from sources.				

Ⓒ **Common Core State Standards**

Writing 1. Write opinion pieces on topics or texts, supporting a point of view with reasons and information. **Writing 9.** Draw evidence from literary or informational texts to support analysis, reflection, and research. **Writing 9.a.** Apply grade 4 Reading standards to literature (e.g., "Describe in depth a character, setting, or event in a story or drama, drawing on specific details in the text [e.g., a character's thoughts, words, or actions].").

Write Like a Reporter
Argumentative Paragraph

Student Prompt Reread *Horse Heroes*. Then look at p. 265, which states, "The teams risked death together on a daily basis." Does the author successfully support this claim in the rest of the selection? List the related details that the author presents. In a one-paragraph argument, state your opinion and support it with reasons and details from the text. Use words or phrases such as *for instance, in order to,* and *in addition* to make your reasoning clear.

_____

_____

_____

_____

_____

_____

_____

_____

_____

_____

_____

_____

_____

Write Like a Reporter
Argumentative Paragraph

> **Student Prompt, p. 50** Reread *Horse Heroes.* Then look at p. 265, which
> states, "The teams risked death together on a daily basis." Does the author
> successfully support this claim in the rest of the selection? List the related
> details that the author presents. In a one-paragraph argument, state your
> opinion and support it with reasons and details from the text. Use words
> or phrases such as *for instance, in order to,* and *in addition* to make your
> reasoning clear.

Writing to Sources After students reread *Horse Heroes,* ask them to list the details
that relate to how the Pony Express horses and riders put their lives in danger. Tell
students to base their opinions on details from the text. Remind them to use linking
words and phrases to make their arguments organized and clear.

Students' paragraphs should:

- state an opinion clearly
- provide reasons that are supported by details
- link opinion and reasons using words and phrases related to the opinion stated
- demonstrate strong command of the conventions of standard written English

© Common Core State Standards

Writing 1. Write opinion pieces on topics or texts, supporting a point of view with reasons and information. **Writing 9.** Draw evidence from literary
or informational texts to support analysis, reflection, and research. **Writing 9.b.** Apply grade 4 Reading standards to informational texts (e.g.,
"Explain how an author uses reasons and evidence to support particular points in a text").

Connect the Texts
Argumentative Essay

Student Prompt Reread the part of *Horse Heroes* about the Pony Express on pp. 264–267 and the article about the Pony Express Web site on pp. 278–281. In your opinion, did the e-mails and Web site give you useful new information about the Pony Express? In one paragraph, state your opinion, give reasons, and use facts and details from both readings to support your reasons. Conclude your paragraph with a sentence that clarifies your opinion.

_____

_____

_____

_____

_____

_____

_____

_____

_____

_____

_____

_____

_____

_____

_____

Connect the Texts
Argumentative Essay

> **Student Prompt, p. 52** Reread the part of *Horse Heroes* about the Pony Express on pp. 264–267 and the article about the Pony Express Web site on pp. 278–281. In your opinion, did the e-mails and Web site give you useful new information about the Pony Express? In one paragraph, state your opinion, give reasons, and use facts and details from both readings to support your reasons. Conclude your paragraph with a sentence that clarifies your opinion.

Writing to Sources After students reread the *Horse Heroes* passage, the e-mails, and the information from the Web site, ask them to point out the main facts in the selections. Have them write a one-paragraph argument about whether the Web site gave useful new information about the Pony Express. Students should include evidence from each text to support their opinions. Remind students to clarify their opinions with concluding sentences.

4-point Argument Writing Rubric					
Score	**Statement of Purpose/Focus**	**Organization**	**Development of Evidence**	**Language and Vocabulary**	**Conventions**
4	Opinion is clearly conveyed and well supported; response is focused.	Organization is clear and effective, creating a sense of cohesion.	Evidence is thorough and persuasive, and includes facts and details.	Ideas are clearly and effectively conveyed, using precise language and/or domain-specific vocabulary.	Command of conventions is strongly demonstrated.
3	Opinion is clear, adequately supported; response is generally focused.	Organization is clear, though minor flaws may be present and some ideas may be disconnected.	Evidence is adequate and includes facts and details.	Ideas are adequately conveyed, using both precise and more general language; may include domain-specific vocabulary.	Command of conventions is sufficiently demonstrated.
2	Opinion is somewhat supported; response may lack focus or include unnecessary material.	Organization is inconsistent, and flaws are apparent.	Evidence is uneven or incomplete; insufficient use of facts and details.	Ideas are unevenly conveyed, using overly-simplistic language; lack of domain-specific vocabulary.	Command of conventions is uneven.
1	The response may be confusing, unfocused; opinion not sufficiently supported.	Organization is poor or nonexistent.	Evidence is poor or nonexistent.	Ideas are conveyed in a vague, unclear, or confusing manner.	There is very little command of conventions.
0	The response shows no evidence of the ability to construct a coherent opinion essay using information from sources.				

Ⓒ Common Core State Standards

Writing 1. Write opinion pieces on topics or texts, supporting a point of view with reasons and information. **Writing 9.** Draw evidence from literary or informational texts to support analysis, reflection, and research. **Writing 9.b.** Apply grade 4 Reading standards to informational texts (e.g., "Explain how an author uses reasons and evidence to support particular points in a text").

Write Like a Reporter
Argumentative Paragraph

Student Prompt Reread *So You Want to Be President?* and make careful notes of facts and details. In your opinion, which two facts in the passage are most important to know if you want to become President someday? In a one-paragraph argument, state your opinion and support it with reasons and details from the text. Conclude your argument with a sentence that sums up your evidence and your opinion.

_____

_____

_____

_____

_____

_____

_____

_____

_____

_____

_____

_____

_____

_____

_____

Write Like a Reporter
Argumentative Paragraph

> **Student Prompt, p. 54** Reread *So You Want to Be President?* and make careful notes of facts and details. In your opinion, which two facts in the passage are most important to know if you want to become President someday? In a one-paragraph argument, state your opinion and support it with reasons and details from the text. Conclude your argument with a sentence that sums up your evidence and your opinion.

Writing to Sources After students reread the passage, have them list the main facts and details. Each student should choose the two facts he or she believes are most important for potential presidential candidates to know. Guide students to clearly state their opinions and support them with evidence from the text. Remind students to write a concluding sentence that effectively sums up their evidence and reasoning.

Students' paragraphs should:

- clearly state an opinion
- provide reasons that are supported by details
- provide a concluding sentence that follows from the opinion presented
- demonstrate strong command of the conventions of standard written English

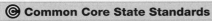 **Common Core State Standards**

Writing 1. Write opinion pieces on topics or texts, supporting a point of view with reasons and information. **Writing 9.** Draw evidence from literary or informational texts to support analysis, reflection, and research. **Writing 9.b.** Apply grade 4 Reading standards to informational texts (e.g., "Explain how an author uses reasons and evidence to support particular points in a text").

Connect the Texts
Argumentative Essay

Student Prompt Reread *So You Want to Be President?* and "Our National Parks." On pp. 300–301, the author describes some qualities the Presidents have had in common. In your opinion, which qualities also describe the Presidents who established the national parks? State your opinion in one paragraph and use facts and details from each passage to support your opinion. Write a concluding sentence to sum up your reasoning.

_____

_____

_____

_____

_____

_____

_____

_____

_____

_____

_____

_____

_____

_____

Connect the Texts
Argumentative Essay

Student Prompt, p. 56 Reread *So You Want to Be President?* and "Our National Parks." On pp. 300–301, the author describes some qualities the Presidents have had in common. In your opinion, which qualities also describe the Presidents who established the national parks? State your opinion in one paragraph and use facts and details from each passage to support your opinion. Write a concluding sentence to sum up your reasoning.

Writing to Sources After students reread the texts, guide them to concentrate on the qualities that Presidents have in common (pp. 300–301) and then infer why Presidents Lincoln and Grant might have set aside land for the national parks. Students should write a one-paragraph argument linking qualities from *So You Want to Be President?* and the text about the parks. Students should include evidence from each text to support their opinions. Remind students to include a concluding sentence to sum up their arguments.

4-point Argument Writing Rubric					
Score	**Statement of Purpose/Focus**	**Organization**	**Development of Evidence**	**Language and Vocabulary**	**Conventions**
4	Opinion is clearly conveyed and well supported; response is focused.	Organization is clear and effective, creating a sense of cohesion.	Evidence is thorough and persuasive, and includes facts and details.	Ideas are clearly and effectively conveyed, using precise language and/or domain-specific vocabulary.	Command of conventions is strongly demonstrated.
3	Opinion is clear, adequately supported; response is generally focused.	Organization is clear, though minor flaws may be present and some ideas may be disconnected.	Evidence is adequate and includes facts and details.	Ideas are adequately conveyed, using both precise and more general language; may include domain-specific vocabulary.	Command of conventions is sufficiently demonstrated.
2	Opinion is somewhat supported; response may lack focus or include unnecessary material.	Organization is inconsistent, and flaws are apparent.	Evidence is uneven or incomplete; insufficient use of facts and details.	Ideas are unevenly conveyed, using overly-simplistic language; lack of domain-specific vocabulary.	Command of conventions is uneven.
1	The response may be confusing, unfocused; opinion not sufficiently supported.	Organization is poor or nonexistent.	Evidence is poor or nonexistent.	Ideas are conveyed in a vague, unclear, or confusing manner.	There is very little command of conventions.
0	The response shows no evidence of the ability to construct a coherent opinion essay using information from sources.				

© Common Core State Standards

Writing 1. Write opinion pieces on topics or texts, supporting a point of view with reasons and information. **Writing 9.** Draw evidence from literary or informational texts to support analysis, reflection, and research. **Writing 9.b.** Apply grade 4 Reading standards to informational texts (e.g., "Explain how an author uses reasons and evidence to support particular points in a text").

Prove It!
Argumentative Essay

The Role of Teamwork

Argumentative Essay

In this unit, students have had the opportunity to write in the argument mode. Remind students of texts and writing tasks (such as Write Like a Reporter and Connect the Texts) in which they have encountered and practiced argumentative writing.

Key Features of an Argumentative Essay

- introduces a topic and states an opinion clearly
- includes sound reasoning supported by facts and details
- includes words and phrases to effectively link reasons for opinions
- is organized so that related ideas are grouped to best serve the writer's purpose
- has a conclusion related to the opinions presented

Writing Task Overview

Each unit writing task provides students with an opportunity to write to sources. To successfully complete the task, students must analyze, synthesize, and evaluate multiple complex texts and create their own written responses.

The Role of Teamwork

Part 1: Students will reread and take notes on the selected sources. They will then respond to several questions about these sources and discuss their written responses with partners or in small groups.

Part 2: Students will work individually to plan, write, and revise their own argumentative essay.

Scorable Products: evidence-based short responses, an argumentative essay

The Role of Teamwork: Writing Task – Short Response

Teacher Directions:

1. **Introduce the Sources** Refer students to the following texts in the Student Edition:

   1. *Coyote School News,* pp. 202–219

   2. *Scene Two,* pp. 234–247

   3. *Horse Heroes,* pp. 262–273

   Explain to students that they will need to draw evidence and support from the texts above in order to answer evidence-based short response questions and to write an argumentative essay. Students should take notes and categorize information as they closely reread the texts. Students should be given paper or a relevant graphic organizer from the TR DVD for note-taking.

2. **Provide Student Directions and Scoring Information (p. 62)** Answer any task-related questions students may have. If necessary, provide additional paper for students to write their responses.

3. **Initiate the Writing Task** If you are timing this part of the task, you may wish to alert students when half the allotted time has elapsed and again when 5 minutes remain.

4. **Facilitate Collaboration** After students have completed their written responses to the evidence-based short response questions, assign students to small groups to discuss their responses. As needed, provide rules and strategies for students to express ideas as well as to link to and build on those of their classmates.

© **Common Core State Standards**

Writing 1. Write opinion pieces on topics or texts, supporting a point of view with reasons and information. **Speaking/Listening 1.** Engage effectively in a range of collaborative discussions (one-on-one, in groups, and teacher-led) with diverse partners on *grade 4 topics and texts,* building on others' ideas and expressing their own clearly. **(Also Writing 1.a., Writing 1.b., Writing 1.c., Writing 1.d.)**

Scoring Information

Use the following 2-point scoring rubrics to evaluate students' answers to the evidence-based short response questions.

1. Using details from the texts, describe the key role teamwork played in each selection.

	Analysis Rubric	
2	The response: • demonstrates the ability to analyze similarities and differences among the texts • includes specific details that make reference to the texts	
1	The response: • demonstrates limited ability to analyze similarities and differences among the texts • includes some details that make reference to the texts	
0	A response gets no credit if it demonstrates no ability to analyze similarities and differences among the texts or includes no relevant details from the texts.	

2. Think about how Monchi worked with his classmates and family, how the student playwrights worked as a team, and how the Pony Express riders and others teamed with their horses. Contrast the way they did so to achieve something, complete a task, or meet a challenge. Support your answer with key words and phrases from the texts.

	Synthesis Rubric	
2	The response: • demonstrates the ability to synthesize information from the sources in order to describe desirable qualities in a team member • includes specific details that make reference to the texts	
1	The response: • demonstrates limited ability to synthesize information from the sources in order to describe desirable qualities in a team member • includes some details that make reference to the texts	
0	A response gets no credit if it demonstrates no ability to synthesize information from the sources or includes no relevant details from the texts.	

3. Consider what you have read about people working as teams. Evaluate whether teamwork is more useful or more challenging in accomplishing a difficult task. Use details from each text to support your opinion.

	Evaluation Rubric	
2	The response: • gives sufficient evidence of the ability to evaluate texts in order to judge how useful and how challenging teamwork is • includes specific details that make reference to the texts	
1	The response: • gives limited evidence of the ability to evaluate texts in order to judge how useful and how challenging teamwork is • includes some details that make reference to the texts	
0	A response gets no credit if it provides no evidence of the ability to evaluate texts or includes no relevant details from the texts.	

Ⓒ **Common Core State Standards**

Writing 8. Recall relevant information from experiences or gather relevant information from print and digital sources; take notes and categorize information, and provide a list of sources. **Writing 9.** Draw evidence from literary or informational texts to support analysis, reflection, and research.

The Role of Teamwork
Writing Task – Short Response

Student Directions:

Your Assignment You will reread several selections from Unit 2 and take notes on these sources. Then you will answer three questions about these materials. You may refer to your notes or to any of the sources as often as you like.

Sources

1. *Coyote School News,* pp. 202–219

2. *Scene Two,* pp. 234–247

3. *Horse Heroes,* pp. 262–273

Be sure to read closely and take good notes. Your sources and notes will be the basis for writing your own argumentative essay in the second half of this writing task.

Evidence-Based Short Response Questions Answer the short response questions on the lines provided below each question. Your answers to these questions will be scored. Be sure to base your answers on the sources you have just read. Remember that you may refer back to your notes or to any of the sources.

After you have answered the questions, you will discuss your responses with a partner or within a small group. Your teacher will let you know when to begin the discussion part of this task.

Scoring Information Your responses will be scored based on how you demonstrate the ability to:

- compare information across texts
- include relevant evidence from sources
- identify, analyze, synthesize, and evaluate information from sources
- distinguish key details and support from irrelevant information

Evidence-Based Short Response Questions

1. Using details from the texts, describe the key role teamwork played in each selection.

_____

_____

_____

_____

2. Think about how Monchi worked with his classmates and family, how the student playwrights worked as a team, and how the Pony Express riders and others teamed with their horses. Contrast the way they did so to achieve something, complete a task, or meet a challenge. Support your answer with key words and phrases from the texts.

_____

_____

_____

_____

3. Consider what you have read about people working as teams. Evaluate whether teamwork is more useful or more challenging in accomplishing a difficult task. Use details from each text to support your opinion.

_____

_____

_____

_____

Collaborative Discussion

After you have written your responses to the questions, discuss your ideas.

The Role of Teamwork: Writing Task – Argumentative Essay

Teacher Directions:

1. **Provide Student Directions and Scoring Information (p. 66)** Explain to students that they will now review their notes and sources, and plan, draft, and revise their argumentative essays. Although they may use their notes and sources, they must work alone. Students will be allowed to look back at the answers they wrote for the short response questions, but they are not allowed to make changes to those answers. Have students read the directions for the argumentative essay and answer any task-related questions they may have. Students should be given paper on which to write their argumentative essays.

2. **Initiate the Writing** If you are timing this part of the task, you may wish to suggest approximate times for students to begin writing and revising. If students wish to continue writing rather than revising, allow them to do so. Alert students when 5 minutes remain.

3. **Scoring Information** Use the scoring rubric on the next page to evaluate students' argumentative essays.

4. **Essay Prompt** Do people do a better job when they are part of a team or when they are working alone? Use what you learned by reading about teamwork in *Coyote School News, Scene Two,* and *Horse Heroes* to write an argumentative essay in which you state your opinion about whether teamwork or individual work is more productive. Support your opinion with details from the three texts.

4-point Argument Writing Rubric					
Score	Statement of Purpose/Focus	Organization	Development of Evidence	Language and Vocabulary	Conventions
4	Opinion is clearly conveyed and well supported; response is focused.	Organization is clear and effective, creating a sense of cohesion.	Evidence is thorough and persuasive, and includes facts and details.	Ideas are clearly and effectively conveyed, using precise language and/or domain-specific vocabulary.	Command of conventions is strongly demonstrated.
3	Opinion is clear, adequately supported; response is generally focused.	Organization is clear, though minor flaws may be present and some ideas may be disconnected.	Evidence is adequate and includes facts and details.	Ideas are adequately conveyed, using both precise and more general language; may include domain-specific vocabulary.	Command of conventions is sufficiently demonstrated.
2	Opinion is somewhat supported; response may lack focus or include unnecessary material.	Organization is inconsistent, and flaws are apparent.	Evidence is uneven or incomplete; insufficient use of facts and details.	Ideas are unevenly conveyed, using overly-simplistic language; lack of domain-specific vocabulary.	Command of conventions is uneven.
1	The response may be confusing, unfocused; opinion not sufficiently supported.	Organization is poor or nonexistent.	Evidence is poor or nonexistent.	Ideas are conveyed in a vague, unclear, or confusing manner.	There is very little command of conventions.
0	The response shows no evidence of the ability to construct a coherent opinion essay using information from sources.				

Common Core State Standards

Writing 1. Write opinion pieces on topics or texts, supporting a point of view with reasons and information. **Writing 9.** Draw evidence from literary or informational texts to support analysis, reflection, and research. **Writing 10.** Write routinely over extended time frames (time for research, reflection, and revision) and shorter time frames (a single sitting or a day or two) for a range of discipline-specific tasks, purposes, and audiences. **(Also Writing 1.a., Writing 1.b.)**

The Role of Teamwork
Writing Task – Argumentative Essay

Student Directions:

Your Assignment Now you will review your notes and sources, and plan, draft, and revise your argumentative essay. While you may use your notes and refer to the sources, you must work on your own. You may also refer to the answers you wrote to earlier questions, but you cannot change those answers.

Argumentative Essay Prompt Do people do a better job when they are part of a team or when they are working alone? Use what you learned by reading about teamwork in *Coyote School News, Scene Two,* and *Horse Heroes* to write an argumentative essay in which you state your opinion about whether teamwork or individual work is more productive. Support your opinion with details from the three texts.

Scoring Information Your argumentative essay will be assigned a score for

1 **Focus** – how clearly you introduce your topic and state your opinion

2 **Organization** – how well your essay groups related ideas together, linking your opinion and reasons

3 **Elaboration** – how well you provide sound reasoning supported by specific details

4 **Language and Vocabulary** – how well you link ideas and use precise language

5 **Conventions** – how well you follow the rules of usage, punctuation, capitalization, and spelling

Now begin work on your argumentative essay. Try to manage your time carefully so that you can

• plan your argumentative essay

• write your argumentative essay

• revise and edit for a final draft

The Role of Teamwork: Writing Task – Argumentative Essay

Teacher Directions:

1. Publish Explain to students that publishing their writing is the last step in the writing process. If time permits, have students review one another's compositions and discuss any comments their classmates have. Offer students suggestions for how to publish their work, such as in a school newspaper, wiki, or blog post. Encourage students to use the Internet to share their work with others.

2. Present Have students present their argumentative essays to the class. Use the list below to offer students some tips on listening and speaking.

While Listening to a Classmate...

- Face the speaker to listen attentively.
- Take notes on what the speaker says.
- Identify and discuss the reasons and evidence the speaker presents.

While Speaking to Classmates...

- Determine your purpose for speaking.
- Have good posture and eye contact.
- Speak at an appropriate pace.

Things to Do Together...

- Ask and answer questions with detail.
- Clarify or follow up on information presented.
- Contribute to the discussion and expand on each other's ideas.

Ⓒ **Common Core State Standards**

Writing 6. With some guidance and support from adults, use technology, including the Internet, to produce and publish writing as well as to interact and collaborate with others; demonstrate sufficient command of keyboarding skills to type a minimum of one page in a single sitting. **Speaking/ Listening 1.b.** Follow agreed-upon rules for discussions and carry out assigned roles. **Speaking/Listening 1.c.** Pose and respond to specific questions to clarify or follow up on information, and make comments that contribute to the discussion and link to the remarks of others. **Speaking/ Listening 3.** Identify the reasons and evidence a speaker provides to support particular points.

Unit 3 Patterns in Nature

Writing Focus: Informative/Explanatory

Write Like a Reporter
Informative/Explanatory Paragraph

Student Prompt Reread the selection *The Man Who Named the Clouds*, and write a one-paragraph summary of how Luke Howard developed his system for naming the different types of clouds. Be sure to include facts and concrete details from the text in your paragraph. Use domain-specific vocabulary to explain the topic.

_____

_____

_____

_____

_____

_____

_____

_____

_____

_____

_____

_____

_____

_____

_____

_____

_____

_____

_____

Write Like a Reporter
Informative/Explanatory Paragraph

Student Prompt, p. 70 Reread the selection *The Man Who Named the Clouds*, and write a one-paragraph summary of how Luke Howard developed his system for naming the different types of clouds. Be sure to include facts and concrete details from the text in your paragraph. Use domain-specific vocabulary to explain the topic.

Writing to Sources After students reread the text, have them write a short summary of the main topics, facts, and details presented. Remind students to include domain-specific language when referring to the process Luke uses to name the clouds. Their summaries should present the information clearly in sequence and provide concrete details and descriptions from the text.

Students' paragraphs should:

- introduce the topic clearly
- develop the topic with facts and concrete details
- use domain-specific vocabulary to inform about or explain the topic
- demonstrate strong command of the conventions of standard written English

Ⓒ **Common Core State Standards**

Writing 2. Write informative/explanatory texts to examine a topic and convey ideas and information clearly. **Writing 9.** Draw evidence from literary or informational texts to support analysis, reflection, and research. **Writing 9.b.** Apply grade 4 Reading standards to informational texts (e.g., "Explain how an author uses reasons and evidence to support particular points in a text").

Connect the Texts
Informative/Explanatory Summary

Student Prompt Look back at *The Man Who Named the Clouds* and "My Weather Journal." Write a one-paragraph summary comparing and contrasting the methods Luke and Grace use to study the weather. Be sure to include facts, concrete details, and quotations from both passages as you write your paragraph. Use linking words, such as *another*, *for example*, *also*, and *because*, to make your explanation clear.

_____

_____

_____

_____

_____

_____

_____

_____

_____

_____

_____

_____

_____

_____

_____

Connect the Texts
Informative/Explanatory Summary

> **Student Prompt, p. 72** Look back at *The Man Who Named the Clouds* and "My Weather Journal." Write a one-paragraph summary comparing and contrasting the methods Luke and Grace use to study the weather. Be sure to include facts, concrete details, and quotations from both passages as you write your paragraph. Use linking words, such as *another, for example, also,* and *because,* to make your explanation clear.

Writing to Sources Discuss the methods used to study weather in both passages. Remind students to carefully reread the texts. Ask them to summarize, compare, and contrast the methods in a single paragraph. Students should use concrete details, quotations, and facts from both passages, in addition to linking words and phrases, to make their explanations clear.

		Informative/Explanatory Writing Rubric			
Score	Focus	Organization	Development of Evidence	Language and Vocabulary	Conventions
4	Main idea is clearly conveyed and well supported; response is focused.	Organization is clear and effective, creating a sense of cohesion.	Evidence is relevant and thorough; includes facts and details.	Ideas are clearly and effectively conveyed, using precise language and/or domain-specific vocabulary.	Command of conventions is strongly demonstrated.
3	Main idea is clear, adequately supported; response is generally focused.	Organization is clear, though minor flaws may be present and some ideas may be disconnected.	Evidence is adequate and includes facts and details.	Ideas are adequately conveyed, using both precise and more general language; may include domain-specific vocabulary.	Command of conventions is sufficiently demonstrated.
2	Main idea is somewhat supported; lacks focus or includes unnecessary material.	Organization is inconsistent, and flaws are apparent.	Evidence is uneven or incomplete; insufficient use of facts and details.	Ideas are unevenly conveyed, using overly-simplistic language; lacks domain-specific vocabulary.	Command of conventions is uneven.
1	Response may be confusing, unfocused; main idea insufficiently supported.	Organization is poor or nonexistent.	Evidence is poor or nonexistent.	Ideas are conveyed in a vague, unclear, or confusing manner.	There is very little command of conventions.
0	The response shows no evidence of the ability to construct a coherent explanatory essay using information from sources.				

Ⓒ **Common Core State Standards**

Writing 2. Write informative/explanatory texts to examine a topic and convey ideas and information clearly. **Writing 9.** Draw evidence from literary or informational texts to support analysis, reflection, and research. **Writing 9.b.** Apply grade 4 Reading standards to informational texts (e.g., "Explain how an author uses reasons and evidence to support particular points in a text").

Write Like a Reporter
Informative/Explanatory Paragraph

Student Prompt Reread *Adelina's Whales* and write a one-paragraph summary of the facts about gray whales presented in the reading. Be sure to clearly introduce the topic and include definitions, descriptions, and concrete details about the whales' behavior in your paragraph. Use domain-specific vocabulary to explain the topic.

_____

_____

_____

_____

_____

_____

_____

_____

_____

_____

_____

_____

_____

_____

_____

_____

Write Like a Reporter
Informative/Explanatory Paragraph

Student Prompt, p. 74 Reread *Adelina's Whales* and write a one-paragraph summary of the facts about gray whales presented in the reading. Be sure to clearly introduce the topic and include definitions, descriptions, and concrete details about the whales' behavior in your paragraph. Use domain-specific vocabulary to explain the topic.

Writing to Sources After students reread the selection, have them write a short summary of the main facts and details presented about gray whales. Remind students to include domain-specific language when defining whale parts and behavior. Their summaries should present information clearly in sequence and provide concrete details and descriptions from the text.

Students' paragraphs should:

- introduce the topic clearly
- develop the topic with definitions, facts, and concrete details
- use domain-specific vocabulary to inform about or explain the topic
- demonstrate strong command of the conventions of standard written English

© **Common Core State Standards**

Writing 2. Write informative/explanatory texts to examine a topic and convey ideas and information clearly. **Writing 9.** Draw evidence from literary or informational texts to support analysis, reflection, and research. **Writing 9.b.** Apply grade 4 Reading standards to informational texts (e.g., "Explain how an author uses reasons and evidence to support particular points in a text").

Connect the Texts
Informative/Explanatory Summary

Student Prompt Look back at *Adelina's Whales* and "Sea Animals on the Move." Write a one-paragraph summary comparing and contrasting facts about the migration habits of gray whales and one of the other sea animals from the article. Be sure to include facts and concrete details from both passages as you write your summary. Use linking words, such as *another, for example, also,* and *because,* to make your explanation clear.

_____

_____

_____

_____

_____

_____

_____

_____

_____

_____

_____

_____

_____

_____

_____

Connect the Texts
Informative/Explanatory Summary

Student Prompt, p. 76 Look back at *Adelina's Whales* and "Sea Animals on the Move." Write a one-paragraph summary comparing and contrasting facts about the migration habits of gray whales and one of the other sea animals from the article. Be sure to include facts and concrete details from both passages as you write your summary. Use linking words, such as *another, for example, also,* and *because,* to make your explanation clear.

Writing to Sources Discuss migration with students and have them choose one of the animals presented in "Sea Animals on the Move" to compare and contrast with the gray whales in *Adelina's Whales.* Remind students to reread the passages carefully and choose facts and details to use in their summaries. Students should also incorporate linking words and phrases to make their explanations clear.

Informative/Explanatory Writing Rubric				
Score	**Focus**	**Organization**	**Development of Evidence**	**Language and Vocabulary**	**Conventions**
4	Main idea is clearly conveyed and well supported; response is focused.	Organization is clear and effective, creating a sense of cohesion.	Evidence is relevant and thorough; includes facts and details.	Ideas are clearly and effectively conveyed, using precise language and/or domain-specific vocabulary.	Command of conventions is strongly demonstrated.
3	Main idea is clear, adequately supported; response is generally focused.	Organization is clear, though minor flaws may be present and some ideas may be disconnected.	Evidence is adequate and includes facts and details.	Ideas are adequately conveyed, using both precise and more general language; may include domain-specific vocabulary.	Command of conventions is sufficiently demonstrated.
2	Main idea is somewhat supported; lacks focus or includes unnecessary material.	Organization is inconsistent, and flaws are apparent.	Evidence is uneven or incomplete; insufficient use of facts and details.	Ideas are unevenly conveyed, using overly-simplistic language; lacks domain-specific vocabulary.	Command of conventions is uneven.
1	Response may be confusing, unfocused; main idea insufficiently supported.	Organization is poor or nonexistent.	Evidence is poor or nonexistent.	Ideas are conveyed in a vague, unclear, or confusing manner.	There is very little command of conventions.
0	The response shows no evidence of the ability to construct a coherent explanatory essay using information from sources.				

© Common Core State Standards

Writing 2. Write informative/explanatory texts to examine a topic and convey ideas and information clearly. **Writing 9.** Draw evidence from literary or informational texts to support analysis, reflection, and research. **Writing 9.b.** Apply grade 4 Reading standards to informational texts (e.g., "Explain how an author uses reasons and evidence to support particular points in a text").

Write Like a Reporter
Informative/Explanatory Paragraph

Student Prompt Based on rereading the story *How Night Came from the Sea*, write a one-paragraph summary of how night came to be. Your paragraph should begin with a general observation. Then focus on describing the characters and events in the story. Include concrete details and descriptions from the text. Use linking words such as *another, for example, also,* and *because* to help explain the topic.

_____

_____

_____

_____

_____

_____

_____

_____

_____

_____

_____

_____

_____

_____

Write Like a Reporter
Informative/Explanatory Paragraph

Student Prompt, p. 78 Based on rereading the story *How Night Came from the Sea*, write a one-paragraph summary of how night came to be. Your paragraph should begin with a general observation. Then focus on describing the characters and events in the story. Include concrete details and descriptions from the text. Use linking words such as *another, for example, also,* and *because* to help explain the topic.

Writing to Sources Ask students to reread the passage and pay close attention to details of the plot. Remind them to begin with a general observation and then focus on description. Have them include concrete details and descriptions of events and characters from the story in their summaries. Also have them use linking words to clearly explain the sequence and meaning of events.

Students' paragraphs should:

- provide a general observation and focus
- develop the topic with concrete details and other information and examples related to the topic
- link ideas within and across categories of information using words and phrases
- demonstrate strong command of the conventions of standard written English

© Common Core State Standards

Writing 2. Write informative/explanatory texts to examine a topic and convey ideas and information clearly. **Writing 9.** Draw evidence from literary or informational texts to support analysis, reflection, and research. **Writing 9.a.** Apply grade 4 Reading standards to literature (e.g., "Describe in depth a character, setting, or event in a story or drama, drawing on specific details in the text [e.g., a character's thoughts, words, or actions].").

Connect the Texts
Compare-Contrast Paragraph

Student Prompt Look back at *How Night Came from the Sea* and "The Ant and the Bear." Write a paragraph comparing and contrasting the two myths. Be sure to consider the main events in each passage as you write your paragraph. Include facts and concrete details from both readings. Use precise language in your explanation so that your points are clear.

_____

_____

_____

_____

_____

_____

_____

_____

_____

_____

_____

_____

_____

Connect the Texts
Compare-Contrast Paragraph

Student Prompt, p. 80 Look back at *How Night Came from the Sea* and "The Ant and the Bear." Write a paragraph comparing and contrasting the two myths. Be sure to consider the main events in each passage as you write your paragraph. Include facts and concrete details from both readings. Use precise language in your explanation so that your points are clear.

Writing to Sources Discuss the genre of myth and ask students to summarize the main points of each myth they read. Remind students to reread the passages carefully and then compare and contrast the main events, details, and facts presented in each. Students should use precise language to make their explanations organized and clear.

			Informative/Explanatory Writing Rubric		
Score	**Focus**	**Organization**	**Development of Evidence**	**Language and Vocabulary**	**Conventions**
4	Main idea is clearly conveyed and well supported; response is focused.	Organization is clear and effective, creating a sense of cohesion.	Evidence is relevant and thorough; includes facts and details.	Ideas are clearly and effectively conveyed, using precise language and/or domain-specific vocabulary.	Command of conventions is strongly demonstrated.
3	Main idea is clear, adequately supported; response is generally focused.	Organization is clear, though minor flaws may be present and some ideas may be disconnected.	Evidence is adequate and includes facts and details.	Ideas are adequately conveyed, using both precise and more general language; may include domain-specific vocabulary.	Command of conventions is sufficiently demonstrated.
2	Main idea is somewhat supported; lacks focus or includes unnecessary material.	Organization is inconsistent, and flaws are apparent.	Evidence is uneven or incomplete; insufficient use of facts and details.	Ideas are unevenly conveyed, using overly-simplistic language; lacks domain-specific vocabulary.	Command of conventions is uneven.
1	Response may be confusing, unfocused; main idea insufficiently supported.	Organization is poor or nonexistent.	Evidence is poor or nonexistent.	Ideas are conveyed in a vague, unclear, or confusing manner.	There is very little command of conventions.
0	The response shows no evidence of the ability to construct a coherent explanatory essay using information from sources.				

Ⓒ Common Core State Standards

Writing 2. Write informative/explanatory texts to examine a topic and convey ideas and information clearly. **Writing 9.** Draw evidence from literary or informational texts to support analysis, reflection, and research. **Writing 9.a.** Apply grade 4 Reading standards to literature (e.g., "Describe in depth a character, setting, or event in a story or drama, drawing on specific details in the text [e.g., a character's thoughts, words, or actions].").

Write Like a Reporter
Informative/Explanatory Paragraph

Student Prompt Reread the expository text *Eye of the Storm,* and write a one-paragraph summary of the tasks, risks, and rewards that Warren and other storm chasers experience when they record dangerous weather. Begin with a general observation, and then focus on the risks and rewards. Include facts, definitions, and concrete details of the events from the text, and use vocabulary from the selection to help explain the topic.

_____

_____

_____

_____

_____

_____

_____

_____

_____

_____

_____

_____

_____

_____

_____

_____

Write Like a Reporter
Informative/Explanatory Paragraph

> **Student Prompt, p. 82** Reread the expository text *Eye of the Storm*, and write a one-paragraph summary of the tasks, risks, and rewards that Warren and other storm chasers experience when they record dangerous weather. Begin with a general observation, and then focus on the risks and rewards. Include facts, definitions, and concrete details of the events from the text, and use vocabulary from the selection to help explain the topic.

Writing to Sources Discuss the dangers and adventures associated with storm chasing. Ask students to reread the passage and list the main events and facts. Remind students to include descriptions of events, facts, and details from the text in their summaries. Students should also use domain-specific vocabulary to make their explanations clear.

Students' paragraphs should:

- provide a general observation or focus
- develop the topic with facts, definitions, and concrete details related to the topic
- use domain-specific vocabulary to inform about or explain the topic
- demonstrate strong command of the conventions of standard written English

ⓒ **Common Core State Standards**

Writing 2. Write informative/explanatory texts to examine a topic and convey ideas and information clearly. **Writing 9.** Draw evidence from literary or informational texts to support analysis, reflection, and research. **Writing 9.b.** Apply grade 4 Reading standards to informational texts (e.g., "Explain how an author uses reasons and evidence to support particular points in a text").

Connect the Texts
Informative/Explanatory Summary

Student Prompt Look back at *Eye of the Storm* and "Severe Weather Safety." Write a one-paragraph summary of *Eye of the Storm* and the ways in which Web sites might be helpful in learning more about storm chasing and dangerous weather. Be sure to introduce the topic clearly. Include facts, definitions, and concrete details from both readings. Use and define vocabulary in your summary so your points are clear.

_____

_____

_____

_____

_____

_____

_____

_____

_____

_____

_____

_____

_____

_____

Connect the Texts
Informative/Explanatory Summary

Student Prompt, p. 84 Look back at *Eye of the Storm* and "Severe Weather Safety." Write a one-paragraph summary of *Eye of the Storm* and the ways in which Web sites might be helpful in learning more about storm chasing and dangerous weather. Be sure to introduce the topic clearly. Include facts, definitions, and concrete details from both readings. Use and define vocabulary in your summary so your points are clear.

Writing to Sources Discuss *Eye of the Storm* and the "Severe Weather Safety" Internet search with students. Ask students to compare and contrast the information in the passage with the information on the Web sites they find. Students should use concrete details, definitions, and facts found in both sources. Remind students to use and define domain-specific language in their explanations.

Informative/Explanatory Writing Rubric				
Score	Focus	Organization	Development of Evidence	Language and Vocabulary	Conventions
4	Main idea is clearly conveyed and well supported; response is focused.	Organization is clear and effective, creating a sense of cohesion.	Evidence is relevant and thorough; includes facts and details.	Ideas are clearly and effectively conveyed, using precise language and/or domain-specific vocabulary.	Command of conventions is strongly demonstrated.
3	Main idea is clear, adequately supported; response is generally focused.	Organization is clear, though minor flaws may be present and some ideas may be disconnected.	Evidence is adequate and includes facts and details.	Ideas are adequately conveyed, using both precise and more general language; may include domain-specific vocabulary.	Command of conventions is sufficiently demonstrated.
2	Main idea is somewhat supported; lacks focus or includes unnecessary material.	Organization is inconsistent, and flaws are apparent.	Evidence is uneven or incomplete; insufficient use of facts and details.	Ideas are unevenly conveyed, using overly-simplistic language; lacks domain-specific vocabulary.	Command of conventions is uneven.
1	Response may be confusing, unfocused; main idea insufficiently supported.	Organization is poor or nonexistent.	Evidence is poor or nonexistent.	Ideas are conveyed in a vague, unclear, or confusing manner.	There is very little command of conventions.
0	The response shows no evidence of the ability to construct a coherent explanatory essay using information from sources.				

© Common Core State Standards

Writing 2. Write informative/explanatory texts to examine a topic and convey ideas and information clearly. **Writing 9.** Draw evidence from literary or informational texts to support analysis, reflection, and research. **Writing 9.b.** Apply grade 4 Reading standards to informational texts (e.g., "Explain how an author uses reasons and evidence to support particular points in a text").

Write Like a Reporter
Informative/Explanatory Paragraph

Student Prompt Reread *Paul Bunyan* and write a one-paragraph summary of the characters, main events, and details. To introduce the topic, draw a conclusion about how the tall tale explains natural events and formations. Develop the topic using words and phrases such as *another, for example, also,* and *because* to link ideas. Be sure to include descriptions and concrete details from the reading in your paragraph.

_____

_____

_____

_____

_____

_____

_____

_____

_____

_____

_____

_____

_____

Write Like a Reporter
Informative/Explanatory Paragraph

> **Student Prompt, p. 86** Reread *Paul Bunyan* and write a one-paragraph summary of the characters, main events, and details. To introduce the topic, draw a conclusion about how the tall tale explains natural events and formations. Develop the topic using words and phrases such as *another, for example, also,* and *because* to link ideas. Be sure to include descriptions and concrete details from the reading in your paragraph.

Writing to Sources Discuss the purpose of a tall tale. Ask students to reread *Paul Bunyan* and pay close attention to the events and facts described. Invite students to draw conclusions about how specific events in the story are used to describe natural phenomena. Students should include concrete details from the story in their summaries and link ideas using words and phrases.

Students' paragraphs should:
- clearly introduce the topic
- develop the topic with descriptions and concrete details
- link ideas within and across categories of information using words and phrases
- demonstrate strong command of the conventions of standard written English

© Common Core State Standards

Writing 2. Write informative/explanatory texts to examine a topic and convey ideas and information clearly. **Writing 9.** Draw evidence from literary or informational texts to support analysis, reflection, and research. **Writing 9.a.** Apply grade 4 Reading standards to literature (e.g., "Describe in depth a character, setting, or event in a story or drama, drawing on specific details in the text [e.g., a character's thoughts, words, or actions].").

Connect the Texts
Compare-Contrast Paragraph

Student Prompt Look back at p. 444 of *Paul Bunyan* and p. 455 of "A Very Grand Canyon." Write a paragraph that compares and contrasts the main ideas of these passages, especially about what formed the Grand Canyon. Be sure to include main events from both texts as well as facts, definitions, and concrete details. Use and define related vocabulary in your explanation.

_____

_____

_____

_____

_____

_____

_____

_____

_____

_____

_____

_____

_____

_____

_____

_____

Connect the Texts
Compare-Contrast Paragraph

> **Student Prompt, p. 88** Look back at p. 444 of *Paul Bunyan* and p. 455 of "A Very Grand Canyon." Write a paragraph that compares and contrasts the main ideas of these passages, especially about what formed the Grand Canyon. Be sure to include main events from both texts as well as facts, definitions, and concrete details. Use and define related vocabulary in your explanation.

Writing to Sources Discuss the Grand Canyon stories in *Paul Bunyan* and "A Very Grand Canyon." Ask students to compare and contrast the information in the tall tale with the facts presented in the expository text. Students should compare and contrast the main ideas of both passages, using details, definitions, and facts found in the texts. Remind students to use and define domain-specific language as they describe the formation of the Grand Canyon.

Informative/Explanatory Writing Rubric				
Score	Focus	Organization	Development of Evidence	Language and Vocabulary	Conventions
4	Main idea is clearly conveyed and well supported; response is focused.	Organization is clear and effective, creating a sense of cohesion.	Evidence is relevant and thorough; includes facts and details.	Ideas are clearly and effectively conveyed, using precise language and/or domain-specific vocabulary.	Command of conventions is strongly demonstrated.
3	Main idea is clear, adequately supported; response is generally focused.	Organization is clear, though minor flaws may be present and some ideas may be disconnected.	Evidence is adequate and includes facts and details.	Ideas are adequately conveyed, using both precise and more general language; may include domain-specific vocabulary.	Command of conventions is sufficiently demonstrated.
2	Main idea is somewhat supported; lacks focus or includes unnecessary material.	Organization is inconsistent, and flaws are apparent.	Evidence is uneven or incomplete; insufficient use of facts and details.	Ideas are unevenly conveyed, using overly-simplistic language; lacks domain-specific vocabulary.	Command of conventions is uneven.
1	Response may be confusing, unfocused; main idea insufficiently supported.	Organization is poor or nonexistent.	Evidence is poor or nonexistent.	Ideas are conveyed in a vague, unclear, or confusing manner.	There is very little command of conventions.
0	The response shows no evidence of the ability to construct a coherent explanatory essay using information from sources.				

Ⓒ Common Core State Standards

Writing 2. Write informative/explanatory texts to examine a topic and convey ideas and information clearly. **Writing 9.** Draw evidence from literary or informational texts to support analysis, reflection, and research. **Writing 9.a.** Apply grade 4 Reading standards to literature (e.g., "Describe in depth a character, setting, or event in a story or drama, drawing on specific details in the text [e.g., a character's thoughts, words, or actions]."). **Writing 9.b.** Apply grade 4 Reading standards to informational texts (e.g., "Explain how an author uses reasons and evidence to support particular points in a text").

Prove It!
Compare-Contrast Essay

Academic Vocabulary

In a **compare-contrast essay**, a writer explores the similarities and differences between two or more people, places, things, ideas, or events.

ELL

Introduce Genre Write *compare* and *contrast* on the board. Explain that to compare things means to point out how they are alike and to contrast things means to show how they differ. Show two classroom objects and have students tell how they are alike and how they are different.

Patterns in Nature

Informative/Explanatory Compare-Contrast Essay

In this unit, students have read examples of informative/explanatory writing and have had the opportunity to write in this mode. Remind students of texts and writing tasks (such as Write Like a Reporter and Connect the Texts) in which they have encountered and practiced informative/explanatory writing.

Key Features of an Informative/Explanatory Compare-Contrast Essay

- identifies the topic clearly and groups related information about similarities and differences
- develops main ideas with facts, definitions, details, quotations, or other information
- uses signal words such as *also, but, similarly, although, almost,* and *however* to indicate how ideas are linked and to help readers follow explanations
- uses precise language and domain-specific vocabulary
- provides a concluding statement or section to summarize the key ideas

Writing Task Overview

Each unit writing task provides students with an opportunity to write to sources. To successfully complete the task, students must analyze, synthesize, and evaluate multiple complex texts and create their own written response.

Patterns in Nature

Part 1: Students will reread and take notes on the selected sources. They will then respond to several questions about these sources and discuss their written responses with partners or in small groups.

Part 2: Students will work individually to plan, write, and revise their own informative/explanatory essay.

Scorable Products: evidence-based short responses, informative/explanatory compare-contrast essay

Patterns in Nature: Writing Task – Short Response

Teacher Directions:

1. **Introduce the Sources** Refer students to the following texts in the Student Edition:

   1. *The Man Who Named the Clouds,* pp. 322–335

   2. *Adelina's Whales,* pp. 350–361

   3. *Eye of the Storm,* pp. 408–419

   Explain to students that they will need to draw evidence and support from the texts above in order to answer evidence-based short response questions and to write a compare-contrast essay. Students should take notes and categorize information as they closely reread the texts. Students should be given paper or a relevant graphic organizer from the TR DVD for note-taking.

2. **Provide Student Directions and Scoring Information (p. 94)** Answer any task-related questions students may have. If necessary, provide additional paper for students to write their responses.

3. **Initiate the Writing Task** If you are timing this part of the task, you may wish to alert students when half the allotted time has elapsed and again when 5 minutes remain.

4. **Facilitate Collaboration** After students have completed their written responses to the evidence-based short response questions, assign partners or small groups and have them discuss their responses. If students struggle to work together productively, provide them with tips and strategies for expressing their ideas and building on the ideas of others.

© **Common Core State Standards**

Writing 2. Write informative/explanatory texts to examine a topic and convey ideas and information clearly. **Speaking/Listening 1.** Engage effectively in a range of collaborative discussions (one-on-one, in groups, and teacher-led) with diverse partners on *grade 4 topics and texts,* building on others' ideas and expressing their own clearly. **(Also Writing 2.a., Writing 2.b., Writing 2.c., Writing 2.d.)**

Scoring Information

Use the following 2-point scoring rubrics to evaluate students' answers to the evidence-based short response questions.

1. Compare how weather patterns and weather-related events play key roles in the lives of Luke, Adelina, and Warren. Cite examples from the texts.

	Analysis Rubric
2	The response: • demonstrates the ability to analyze similarities and differences among the texts and uses effective transitional strategies • includes specific details that make reference to the texts
1	The response: • demonstrates a limited ability to analyze similarities and differences among the texts and does not use effective transitional strategies • includes some details that make reference to the texts
0	A response receives no credit if it demonstrates no ability to analyze similarities and differences among the texts or includes no relevant details from the texts.

2. Identify the different ways in which Luke, Adelina, and Warren learn about the patterns in nature that interest them. Compare and contrast their methods. Cite evidence from each of the texts.

	Synthesis Rubric
2	The response: • demonstrates the ability to synthesize information about similarities and differences from both texts • includes specific details that make reference to the texts
1	The response: • demonstrates a limited ability to synthesize information about similarities and differences from both texts • includes some details that make reference to the texts
0	A response receives no credit if it demonstrates no ability to synthesize information from the sources or includes no relevant details from the texts.

3. What are the most important ways in which weather patterns and events affect the lives of people and animals? Cite examples from the texts to support your evaluation.

Evaluation Rubric	
2	The response: • demonstrates the ability to evaluate which effects are most important • includes specific details that make reference to the texts
1	The response: • demonstrates a limited ability to evaluate which effects are most important • includes some details that make reference to the texts
0	A response receives no credit if it demonstrates no ability to analyze and evaluate information from the sources or includes no relevant details from the texts.

ⓒ **Common Core State Standards**

Writing 8. Recall relevant information from experiences or gather relevant information from print and digital sources; take notes and categorize information, and provide a list of sources. **Writing 9.** Draw evidence from literary or informational texts to support analysis, reflection, and research.

Patterns in Nature
Writing Task – Short Response

Student Directions:

Your assignment You will reread several selections from Unit 3 and take notes on these sources. Then you will answer three questions about these materials. You may refer to your notes or to any of the sources as often as you like.

Sources

1. *The Man Who Named the Clouds,* pp. 322–335

2. *Adelina's Whales,* pp. 350–361

3. *Eye of the Storm,* pp. 408–419

Be sure to read closely and take good notes. Your sources and notes will be the basis for writing your own compare-contrast essay in the second half of this writing task.

Evidence-Based Short Response Questions Answer the short response questions on the lines provided below each question. Your answers to these questions will be scored. Be sure to base your answers on the sources you have just read. Remember that you may refer back to your notes or to any of the sources.

After you have answered the questions, you will discuss your responses with a partner or within a small group. Your teacher will let you know when to begin the discussion part of this task.

Scoring Information Your responses will be scored based on how you demonstrate the ability to:

- compare and contrast information across texts
- include specific details that highlight similarities and differences
- identify, analyze, synthesize, and evaluate information from the sources
- Use only details and information relevant to your essay

Evidence-Based Short Response Questions

1. Compare how weather patterns and weather-related events play key roles in the lives of Luke, Adelina, and Warren. Cite examples from the texts.

_____

_____

_____

_____

2. Identify the different ways in which Luke, Adelina, and Warren learn about the patterns in nature that interest them. Compare and contrast their methods. Cite evidence from each of the texts.

_____

_____

_____

_____

3. What are the most important ways in which weather patterns and events affect the lives of people and animals? Cite examples from the texts to support your evaluation.

_____

_____

_____

_____

Collaborative Discussion

After you have written your responses to the questions, discuss your ideas. Your teacher will assign you a partner or a small group and let you know when to begin.

Patterns in Nature: Writing Task – Compare-Contrast Essay

Teacher Directions:

1. **Provide Student Directions and Scoring Information (p. 98)** Explain to students that they will now review their notes and sources, and plan, draft, and revise their essays. Although they may use their notes and sources, they must work alone. Students will be allowed to look back at the answers they wrote to the short response questions, but they are not allowed to make changes to those answers. Have students read the directions for the essay and answer any task-related questions they may have. Students should be given paper on which to write their compare-contrast essays.

2. **Initiate the Writing Task** If you are timing this part of the task, you may wish to suggest approximate times for students to begin writing and revising. If students wish to continue writing rather than revising, allow them to do so. Alert students when 5 minutes remain.

3. **Scoring Information** Use the scoring rubric on the next page to evaluate students' compare-contrast essays.

4. **Compare-Contrast Essay Prompt** Use what you have learned from reading *The Man Who Named the Clouds, Adelina's Whales,* and *Eye of the Storm* to write a compare-contrast essay about how different features of weather affect the lives of people and animals. Use facts, details, and examples from the texts to support your ideas. Be sure to follow the conventions of written English.

4-Point Informative/Explanatory Writing Rubric					
Score	**Focus**	**Organization**	**Development of Evidence**	**Language and Vocabulary**	**Conventions**
4	Main idea is clearly conveyed and well supported; essay is focused.	Organization is clear and effective, creating a sense of cohesion.	Evidence is relative and thorough; includes facts and details.	Ideas are clearly and effectively conveyed, using precise language and/or domain-specific vocabulary.	Command of conventions is strongly demonstrated.
3	Main idea is clear and adequately supported; essay is generally focused.	Organization is clear, though minor flaws may be present, and some ideas may be disconnected.	Evidence is adequate and includes facts and details.	Ideas are adequately conveyed, using both precise and more general language; may include domain-specific vocabulary.	Command of conventions is sufficiently demonstrated.
2	Main idea is somewhat supported; lacks focus or includes unnecessary material.	Organization is inconsistent, and flaws are apparent.	Evidence is uneven or incomplete; insufficient use of facts or details.	Ideas are unevenly conveyed, using simplistic language; lacks domain-specific vocabulary.	Command of conventions is uneven.
1	Essay may be confusing or unfocused; main idea insufficiently supported.	Organization is poor or nonexistent.	Evidence is poor or nonexistent.	Ideas are conveyed in a vague, unclear, or confusing manner.	There is very little command of conventions.
0	The response shows no evidence of the ability to construct a coherent informative/explanatory essay using information from sources.				

Ⓒ **Common Core State Standards**

Writing 2. Write informative/explanatory texts to examine a topic and convey ideas and information clearly. **Writing 9.** Draw evidence from literary or informational texts to support analysis, reflection, and research. **(Also Writing 2.a., Writing 2.b., Writing 2.d., Writing 10.)**

Patterns in Nature
Writing Task – Compare-Contrast Essay

Student Directions:

Your assignment Now you will review your notes and sources, and plan, draft, and revise your compare-contrast essay. While you may use your notes and refer to the sources, you must work on your own. You may also refer to the answers you wrote to earlier questions, but you cannot change those answers.

Compare-Contrast Essay Prompt Use what you have learned from reading *The Man Who Named the Clouds, Adelina's Whales,* and *Eye of the Storm* to write a compare-contrast essay about how different features of weather affect the lives of people and animals. Use facts, details, and examples from the texts to support your ideas. Be sure to follow the conventions of written English.

Scoring Information Your compare-contrast essay will be assigned a score for

1. **Focus** – how well you keep your focus and express information clearly

2. **Organization** – whether you stay on topic, group ideas logically, and effectively use signal words to link information

3. **Elaboration** – how effectively and thoroughly you develop your topic and support your ideas with facts, definitions, details, quotations, or other information

4. **Language and Vocabulary** – how well you use precise language and domain-specific vocabulary to express ideas

5. **Conventions** – how well you follow the conventions of grammar, usage, punctuation, capitalization, and spelling

Now begin work on your compare-contrast essay. Try to manage your time carefully so that you can

- plan your compare-contrast essay
- write your compare-contrast essay
- revise and edit for a final draft

Patterns in Nature: Writing Task – Compare-Contrast Essay

Teacher Directions:

1. Publish Explain to students that publishing their writing is the last step in the writing process. If time permits, have students review one another's essays and incorporate any comments their classmates have. Discuss different ways technology can be used to share and publish writing, such as through email, blogs, or wikis.

2. Present Students will now have the option to present their compare-contrast essays. Have them give speeches on their essays in front of the class. Use the list below to offer students some tips on listening and speaking.

While Listening to a Classmate...

- Ignore all distractions and focus your attention on the speaker.
- Face the speaker to listen carefully.
- Watch for facial expressions, tone of voice changes, and gestures that may alert you to key ideas.
- Take notes on the speaker's main ideas.

While Speaking to Classmates...

- Determine your purpose for speaking.
- Make eye contact with your listeners, use good posture, and speak clearly.
- Change your tone of voice or use gestures to emphasize key points.

Things to Do Together...

- Ask and answer questions to clarify ideas and details.
- Build on each other's ideas.

Ⓒ **Common Core State Standards**

Writing 6. With some guidance and support from adults, use technology, including the Internet, to produce and publish writing as well as to interact and collaborate with others; demonstrate sufficient command of keyboarding skills to type a minimum of one page in a single sitting. **Speaking/Listening 1.b.** Follow agreed-upon rules for discussions and carry out assigned roles. **Speaking/Listening 1.c.** Pose and respond to specific questions to clarify or follow up on information, and make comments that contribute to the discussion and link to the remarks of others. **Speaking/Listening 4.** Report on a topic or text, tell a story, or recount an experience in an organized manner, using appropriate facts and relevant, descriptive details to support main ideas or themes; speak clearly at an understandable pace.

Unit 4 Puzzles and Mysteries

Writing Focus: Narrative

Write Like a Reporter
Narrative Paragraph

Student Prompt Reread the story. Pay special attention to the character of Nell as you read. List Nell's strengths as a scientist. Then write a one-paragraph narrative that retells Doyle and Fossey's garbage experiment from Nell's perspective. Use first-person point of view and clearly show the sequence of events as if you are referring to a lab report. Be sure to include dialogue, description, and sensory details based on details in the story.

_____

_____

_____

_____

_____

_____

_____

_____

_____

_____

_____

_____

_____

_____

_____

_____

Write Like a Reporter
Narrative Paragraph

> **Student Prompt, p. 102** Reread the story. Pay special attention to the character of Nell as you read. List Nell's strengths as a scientist. Then write a one-paragraph narrative that retells Doyle and Fossey's garbage experiment from Nell's perspective. Use first-person point of view and clearly show the sequence of events as if you are referring to a lab report. Be sure to include dialogue, description, and sensory details based on details in the story.

Writing to Sources After students reread the passage, have them list Nell's strengths as a scientist. Point out that the original story is told in third-person point of view. Remind them to write their narratives in first person and encourage them to try to sound like Nell. In their narratives, students should retell the steps of the experiment, using transitional words to make the order clear. They should include concrete words and sensory details to convey what the scientists did and observed. Remind students to reread the text carefully and base their descriptions on details from the original story.

Students' paragraphs should:

- orient the reader by establishing a situation
- use description to show the responses of characters to situations
- use sensory details to convey experiences and events precisely
- demonstrate strong command of the conventions of standard written English

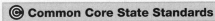
© Common Core State Standards

Writing 3. Write narratives to develop real or imagined experiences or events using effective technique, descriptive details, and clear event sequences. **Writing 9.** Draw evidence from literary or informational texts to support analysis, reflection, and research. **Writing 9.a.** Apply grade 4 Reading standards to literature (e.g., "Describe in depth a character, setting, or event in a story or drama, drawing on specific details in the text [e.g., a character's thoughts, words, or actions].").

Connect the Texts
Narrative Epilogue

Student Prompt Look back at *The Case of the Gasping Garbage* and "Mr. Talberg's Famous Bread Recipe." Review the materials for the bread recipe. Then write a one-paragraph epilogue for the story in which you tell how Gabby, Drake, and Nell make a tasty loaf of bread from the monster in the garbage. Begin your narrative with a sentence that tells why the characters decided to make bread. Use an organized event sequence that is based on details from both texts.

_____

_____

_____

_____

_____

_____

_____

_____

_____

_____

_____

_____

_____

_____

Connect the Texts
Narrative Epilogue

Student Prompt, p. 104 Look back at *The Case of the Gasping Garbage* and "Mr. Talberg's Famous Bread Recipe." Review the materials for the bread recipe. Then write a one-paragraph epilogue for the story in which you tell how Gabby, Drake, and Nell make a tasty loaf of bread from the monster in the garbage. Begin your narrative with a sentence that tells why the characters decided to make bread. Use an organized event sequence that is based on details from both texts.

Writing to Sources Discuss with students how Gabby, Drake, and Nell interact in the story. Explain that an epilogue is a short concluding section that rounds out a story. Then have students write the epilogue as if making bread is a natural consequence of the characters' earlier experiences. Advise them to establish the situation and then use an organized event sequence that builds on dialogue and descriptions in the story.

4-point Narrative Writing Rubric					
Score	Narrative Focus	Organization	Development of Narrative	Language and Vocabulary	Conventions
4	Narrative is clearly focused and developed throughout.	Narrative has a well-developed, logical, easy-to-follow plot.	Narrative includes thorough and effective use of details, dialogue, and description.	Narrative uses precise, concrete sensory language as well as figurative language and/or domain-specific vocabulary.	Narrative has correct grammar, usage, spelling, capitalization, and punctuation.
3	Narrative is mostly focused and developed throughout.	Narrative has a plot, but there may be some lack of clarity and/or unrelated events.	Narrative includes adequate use of details, dialogue and description.	Narrative uses adequate sensory and figurative language and/or domain-specific vocabulary.	Narrative has a few errors but is completely understandable.
2	Narrative is somewhat developed but may occasionally lose focus.	Narrative's plot is difficult to follow, and ideas are not connected well.	Narrative includes only a few details, dialogues, and descriptions.	Language in narrative is not precise or sensory; lacks domain-specific vocabulary.	Narrative has some errors in usage, grammar, spelling and/or punctuation.
1	Narrative may be confusing, unfocused, or too short.	Narrative has little or no apparent plot.	Narrative includes few or no details, dialogue or description.	Language in narrative is vague, unclear, or confusing.	Narrative is hard to follow because of frequent errors.
0	Narrative gets no credit if it does not demonstrate adequate command of narrative writing traits.				

Ⓒ **Common Core State Standards**

Writing 3. Write narratives to develop real or imagined experiences or events using effective technique, descriptive details, and clear event sequences. **Writing 9.** Draw evidence from literary or informational texts to support analysis, reflection, and research. **Writing 9.a.** Apply grade 4 Reading standards to literature (e.g., "Describe in depth a character, setting, or event in a story or drama, drawing on specific details in the text [e.g., a character's thoughts, words, or actions]."). **Writing 9.b.** Apply grade 4 Reading standards to informational texts (e.g., "Explain how an author uses reasons and evidence to support particular points in a text").

Write Like a Reporter
Narrative Paragraph

Student Prompt Reread *Encantado: Pink Dolphin of the Amazon.* As you read, imagine what it would be like to swim alongside one of these animals. Use sensory details and facts from the text to write a one-paragraph, first-person narrative that describes the experience. Report your experience from beginning to end, using transition words to clearly give a sequence of events.

_____

_____

_____

_____

_____

_____

_____

_____

_____

_____

_____

_____

_____

_____

_____

Write Like a Reporter
Narrative Paragraph

> **Student Prompt, p. 106** Reread *Encantado: Pink Dolphin of the Amazon.* As you read, imagine what it would be like to swim alongside one of these animals. Use sensory details and facts from the text to write a one-paragraph, first-person narrative that describes the experience. Report your experience from beginning to end, using transition words to clearly give a sequence of events.

Writing to Sources Before they reread the text, encourage students to write down sensory details about the Amazon and about the pink dolphins that will be useful to them. Suggest that they think of their narratives as short stories with plots that have a beginning, middle, and end. Remind students to select details from the text that will help their audience imagine the experience of swimming with a pink dolphin.

Students' paragraphs should:

- orient the reader by organizing an event sequence that unfolds naturally
- use description to show the responses of characters to situations
- use sensory details to convey experiences and events precisely
- demonstrate strong command of the conventions of standard written English

© **Common Core State Standards**

Writing 3. Write narratives to develop real or imagined experiences or events using effective technique, descriptive details, and clear event sequences. **Writing 9.** Draw evidence from literary or informational texts to support analysis, reflection, and research. **Writing 9.b.** Apply grade 4 Reading standards to informational texts (e.g., "Explain how an author uses reasons and evidence to support particular points in a text").

Connect the Texts
Narrative Dialogue

Student Prompt Look back at pp. 62–63 of *Encantado: Pink Dolphin of the Amazon*. Then review "Mysterious Animals." Choose an animal and write a one-paragraph dialogue between a scientist who studies that animal and a scientist who studies pink dolphins. Introduce your characters and use concrete details from both passages to help your narrative give readers information.

_____

_____

_____

_____

_____

_____

_____

_____

_____

_____

_____

_____

_____

_____

Connect the Texts
Narrative Dialogue

Student Prompt, p. 108 Look back at pp. 62–63 of *Encantado: Pink Dolphin of the Amazon*. Then review "Mysterious Animals." Choose an animal and write a one-paragraph dialogue between a scientist who studies that animal and a scientist who studies pink dolphins. Introduce your characters and use concrete details from both passages to help your narrative give readers information.

Writing to Sources Discuss both expository passages with students and invite them to select an animal from "Mysterious Animals" that they would like to write about. Remind students that they are writing narrative dialogues, not compare-and-contrast essays. They should focus on using the dialogue between their two "scientist" characters to describe concrete details and facts from both passages.

4-point Narrative Writing Rubric					
Score	Narrative Focus	Organization	Development of Narrative	Language and Vocabulary	Conventions
4	Narrative is clearly focused and developed throughout.	Narrative has a well-developed, logical, easy-to-follow plot.	Narrative includes thorough and effective use of details, dialogue, and description.	Narrative uses precise, concrete sensory language as well as figurative language and/or domain-specific vocabulary.	Narrative has correct grammar, usage, spelling, capitalization, and punctuation.
3	Narrative is mostly focused and developed throughout.	Narrative has a plot, but there may be some lack of clarity and/or unrelated events.	Narrative includes adequate use of details, dialogue and description.	Narrative uses adequate sensory and figurative language and/or domain-specific vocabulary.	Narrative has a few errors but is completely understandable.
2	Narrative is somewhat developed but may occasionally lose focus.	Narrative's plot is difficult to follow, and ideas are not connected well.	Narrative includes only a few details, dialogues, and descriptions.	Language in narrative is not precise or sensory; lacks domain-specific vocabulary.	Narrative has some errors in usage, grammar, spelling and/or punctuation.
1	Narrative may be confusing, unfocused, or too short.	Narrative has little or no apparent plot.	Narrative includes few or no details, dialogue or description.	Language in narrative is vague, unclear, or confusing.	Narrative is hard to follow because of frequent errors.
0	Narrative gets no credit if it does not demonstrate adequate command of narrative writing traits.				

ⓒ Common Core State Standards

Writing 3. Write narratives to develop real or imagined experiences or events using effective technique, descriptive details, and clear event sequences. **Writing 9.** Draw evidence from literary or informational texts to support analysis, reflection, and research. **Writing 9.b.** Apply grade 4 Reading standards to informational texts (e.g., "Explain how an author uses reasons and evidence to support particular points in a text").

Name _____

Write Like a Reporter
Narrative Paragraph

Student Prompt Reread pp. 92–94 of *Navajo Code Talkers*. Then write a one-paragraph narrative that presents the meeting between Philip Johnston and Major James E. Jones using dialogue. Use descriptions and details from earlier pages of the passage to make the two men into convincing characters—one who has a problem and another who offers a solution.

_____

_____

_____

_____

_____

_____

_____

_____

_____

_____

_____

_____

_____

_____

Write Like a Reporter
Narrative Paragraph

> **Student Prompt, p. 110** Reread pp. 92–94 of *Navajo Code Talkers*. Then write a one-paragraph narrative that presents the meeting between Philip Johnston and Major James E. Jones using dialogue. Use descriptions and details from earlier pages of the passage to make the two men into convincing characters—one who has a problem and another who offers a solution.

Writing to Sources As students reread pp. 92–94, ask them to write down key pieces of background information that help explain why each man comes to the meeting mentioned on p. 93. Remind students that dialogue contains the words people say as well as text that identifies the speakers. Dialogue may also describe appearances, thoughts and feelings, and nonverbal communication. Have students use details from the text to construct a conversation between the two men.

Students' paragraphs should:

- orient the reader by introducing the characters
- use dialogue to show the responses of characters to situations
- use sensory details to convey experiences and events precisely
- demonstrate strong command of the conventions of standard written English

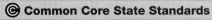
Common Core State Standards

Writing 3. Write narratives to develop real or imagined experiences or events using effective technique, descriptive details, and clear event sequences. **Writing 9.** Draw evidence from literary or informational texts to support analysis, reflection, and research. **Writing 9.b.** Apply grade 4 Reading standards to informational texts (e.g., "Explain how an author uses reasons and evidence to support particular points in a text").

Connect the Texts
Narrative Journal Entry

> **Student Prompt** Reread and retell *Navajo Code Talkers* and "Your Own Secret Language." Then write a journal entry from the point of view of a Navajo soldier who is creating the code using information from the how-to article. Your narrative should include concrete details and facts from both passages.

_____

_____

_____

_____

_____

_____

_____

_____

_____

_____

_____

_____

_____

_____

_____

_____

Connect the Texts
Narrative Journal Entry

> **Student Prompt, p. 112** Reread and retell *Navajo Code Talkers* and "Your Own Secret Language." Then write a journal entry from the point of view of a Navajo soldier who is creating the code using information from the how-to article. Your narrative should include concrete details and facts from both passages.

Writing to Sources Discuss with students how *Navajo Code Talkers* and "Your Own Secret Language" both describe creating a language that outsiders cannot understand. Guide students to retell the story from the point of view of one of the Navajo soldiers. Students should write a journal entry from the soldier's perspective using details from the passage as well as concrete details and facts from the how-to article.

| 4-point Narrative Writing Rubric				
Score	**Narrative Focus**	**Organization**	**Development of Narrative**	**Language and Vocabulary**	**Conventions**
4	Narrative is clearly focused and developed throughout.	Narrative has a well-developed, logical, easy-to-follow plot.	Narrative includes thorough and effective use of details, dialogue, and description.	Narrative uses precise, concrete sensory language as well as figurative language and/or domain-specific vocabulary.	Narrative has correct grammar, usage, spelling, capitalization, and punctuation.
3	Narrative is mostly focused and developed throughout.	Narrative has a plot, but there may be some lack of clarity and/or unrelated events.	Narrative includes adequate use of details, dialogue and description.	Narrative uses adequate sensory and figurative language and/or domain-specific vocabulary.	Narrative has a few errors but is completely understandable.
2	Narrative is somewhat developed but may occasionally lose focus.	Narrative's plot is difficult to follow, and ideas are not connected well.	Narrative includes only a few details, dialogues, and descriptions.	Language in narrative is not precise or sensory; lacks domain-specific vocabulary.	Narrative has some errors in usage, grammar, spelling and/or punctuation.
1	Narrative may be confusing, unfocused, or too short.	Narrative has little or no apparent plot.	Narrative includes few or no details, dialogue or description.	Language in narrative is vague, unclear, or confusing.	Narrative is hard to follow because of frequent errors.
0	Narrative gets no credit if it does not demonstrate adequate command of narrative writing traits.				

Ⓒ **Common Core State Standards**

Writing 3. Write narratives to develop real or imagined experiences or events using effective technique, descriptive details, and clear event sequences. **Writing 9.** Draw evidence from literary or informational texts to support analysis, reflection, and research. **Writing 9.b.** Apply grade 4 Reading standards to informational texts (e.g., "Explain how an author uses reasons and evidence to support particular points in a text").

Write Like a Reporter
Narrative Paragraph

Student Prompt Reread *Seeker of Knowledge*. Pay special attention to how Jean-François spent the years before he went to Egypt preparing for the trip. Select a single time of his life from the biography. Then write a narrative paragraph in which you enter the mind of Jean-François and describe Egypt from his perspective. Use sensory and figurative language to describe the character's thoughts about the place as well as the place itself.

_____

_____

_____

_____

_____

_____

_____

_____

_____

_____

_____

_____

_____

_____

Write Like a Reporter
Narrative Paragraph

Student Prompt, p. 114 Reread *Seeker of Knowledge.* Pay special attention to how Jean-François spent the years before he went to Egypt preparing for the trip. Select a single time of his life from the biography. Then write a narrative paragraph in which you enter the mind of Jean-François and describe Egypt from his perspective. Use sensory and figurative language to describe the character's thoughts about the place as well as the place itself.

Writing to Sources As they reread the biography, have students list sensory and figurative language that gives them strong impressions of Jean-François and Egypt. Remind students to choose one particular time from the biography and take on Jean-François's personality at that time. Point out that they are writing a descriptive narrative, so they can choose to write from either the third-person or first-person point of view.

Students' paragraphs should:

- orient the reader by establishing a situation
- use description to develop experiences and events
- use sensory details to convey experiences and events precisely
- demonstrate strong command of the conventions of standard written English

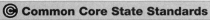
Common Core State Standards

Writing 3. Write narratives to develop real or imagined experiences or events using effective technique, descriptive details, and clear event sequences. **Writing 9.** Draw evidence from literary or informational texts to support analysis, reflection, and research. **Writing 9.b.** Apply grade 4 Reading standards to informational texts (e.g., "Explain how an author uses reasons and evidence to support particular points in a text").

Connect the Texts
Narrative Journal Entry

Student Prompt Reread *Seeker of Knowledge* and "Making Mummies." Notice how "Making Mummies" gives instructions for conducting an Internet search. Imagine that Jean-François is working today to decipher more ancient text. Write a journal entry from his point of view that describes how he uses an Internet search to decipher a hieroglyphic message. Be sure to include details from the biography and "Making Mummies" in your narrative. Use transition words to make the search sequence clear.

_____

_____

_____

_____

_____

_____

_____

_____

_____

_____

_____

_____

_____

_____

_____

_____

Connect the Texts
Narrative Journal Entry

Student Prompt, p. 116 Reread *Seeker of Knowledge* and "Making Mummies." Notice how "Making Mummies" gives instructions for conducting an Internet search. Imagine that Jean-François is working today to decipher more ancient text. Write a journal entry from his point of view that describes how he uses an Internet search to decipher a hieroglyphic message. Be sure to include details from the biography and "Making Mummies" in your narrative. Use transition words to make the search sequence clear.

Writing to Sources Have students use *Seeker of Knowledge* to list the topics Jean-François studied in his quest to decipher hieroglyphics: Egypt, the Rosetta Stone, and the names of pharaohs. Point out the use of keywords and page links in "Making Mummies." As students write their journal entries, remind them to use transition words and phrases to explain what the main character is doing. Encourage them to convey the excitement of the final discovery as they conclude their narratives.

4-point Narrative Writing Rubric					
Score	Narrative Focus	Organization	Development of Narrative	Language and Vocabulary	Conventions
4	Narrative is clearly focused and developed throughout.	Narrative has a well-developed, logical, easy-to-follow plot.	Narrative includes thorough and effective use of details, dialogue, and description.	Narrative uses precise, concrete sensory language as well as figurative language and/or domain-specific vocabulary.	Narrative has correct grammar, usage, spelling, capitalization, and punctuation.
3	Narrative is mostly focused and developed throughout.	Narrative has a plot, but there may be some lack of clarity and/or unrelated events.	Narrative includes adequate use of details, dialogue and description.	Narrative uses adequate sensory and figurative language and/or domain-specific vocabulary.	Narrative has a few errors but is completely understandable.
2	Narrative is somewhat developed but may occasionally lose focus.	Narrative's plot is difficult to follow, and ideas are not connected well.	Narrative includes only a few details, dialogues, and descriptions.	Language in narrative is not precise or sensory; lacks domain-specific vocabulary.	Narrative has some errors in usage, grammar, spelling and/or punctuation.
1	Narrative may be confusing, unfocused, or too short.	Narrative has little or no apparent plot.	Narrative includes few or no details, dialogue or description.	Language in narrative is vague, unclear, or confusing.	Narrative is hard to follow because of frequent errors.
0	Narrative gets no credit if it does not demonstrate adequate command of narrative writing traits.				

Ⓒ **Common Core State Standards**

Writing 3. Write narratives to develop real or imagined experiences or events using effective technique, descriptive details, and clear event sequences. **Writing 9.** Draw evidence from literary or informational texts to support analysis, reflection, and research. **Writing 9.b.** Apply grade 4 Reading standards to informational texts (e.g., "Explain how an author uses reasons and evidence to support particular points in a text").

Write Like a Reporter
Narrative Paragraph

Student Prompt Reread *Encyclopedia Brown*. Pay particular attention to the three suspects described on pp. 151–153. Because Encyclopedia does his detecting with his mind, ask yourself what makes him suspect Sam Maine instead of the other two characters who had access to the salamander. Write a narrative, first-person paragraph from Encyclopedia's point of view, explaining why you asked your pointed question about Sam. Make sure your narrative agrees with the sequence of events in the story.

_____

_____

_____

_____

_____

_____

_____

_____

_____

_____

_____

_____

_____

_____

_____

Write Like a Reporter
Narrative Paragraph

> **Student Prompt, 118** Reread *Encyclopedia Brown.* Pay particular attention to the three suspects described on pp. 151–153. Because Encyclopedia does his detecting with his mind, ask yourself what makes him suspect Sam Maine instead of the other two characters who had access to the salamander. Write a narrative, first-person paragraph from Encyclopedia's point of view, explaining why you asked your pointed question about Sam. Make sure your narrative agrees with the sequence of events in the story.

Writing to Sources Before they reread the story, ask students what they think Encyclopedia Brown would be like as a real person. Then point out that they will write a narrative from this character's point of view. Remind students to use details in the story to explain Encyclopedia's thought process. Advise them to use transition words to clarify the chronology of those thoughts.

Students' paragraphs should:

- orient the reader by establishing a situation
- use descriptive language to develop experiences and events
- use concrete words and phrases to convey experiences and events
- demonstrate strong command of the conventions of standard written English

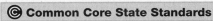

Common Core State Standards

Writing 3. Write narratives to develop real or imagined experiences or events using effective technique, descriptive details, and clear event sequences. **Writing 9.** Draw evidence from literary or informational texts to support analysis, reflection, and research. **Writing 9.a.** Apply grade 4 Reading standards to literature (e.g., "Describe in depth a character, setting, or event in a story or drama, drawing on specific details in the text [e.g., a character's thoughts, words, or actions].").

Connect the Texts
Narrative Paragraph

Student Prompt Review "Young Detectives of Potterville Middle School" and then look back at *Encyclopedia Brown*. Invite the young detectives to solve the mystery of Fred's disappearance. Use details from p. 161 of "Young Detectives" and facts from p. 155 of *Encyclopedia Brown* to choose effective tools for the forensic investigation. Then write a narrative paragraph in which you describe the young detectives and their investigation in detail.

_____

_____

_____

_____

_____

_____

_____

_____

_____

_____

_____

_____

_____

_____

Connect the Texts
Narrative Paragraph

Student Prompt, p. 120 Review "Young Detectives of Potterville Middle School" and then look back at *Encyclopedia Brown*. Invite the young detectives to solve the mystery of Fred's disappearance. Use details from p. 161 of "Young Detectives" and facts from p. 155 of *Encyclopedia Brown* to choose effective tools for the forensic investigation. Then write a narrative paragraph in which you describe the young detectives and their investigation in detail.

Writing to Sources After they revisit the story and the article, ask students to brainstorm about forensic evidence the thief might have left at the scene of Fred's abduction—in the back room of the Den of Darkness or on Fred himself. Remind students to incorporate details from both readings in their imaginary elaboration of the forensic investigation.

			4-point Narrative Writing Rubric		
Score	Narrative Focus	Organization	Development of Narrative	Language and Vocabulary	Conventions
4	Narrative is clearly focused and developed throughout.	Narrative has a well-developed, logical, easy-to-follow plot.	Narrative includes thorough and effective use of details, dialogue, and description.	Narrative uses precise, concrete sensory language as well as figurative language and/or domain-specific vocabulary.	Narrative has correct grammar, usage, spelling, capitalization, and punctuation.
3	Narrative is mostly focused and developed throughout.	Narrative has a plot, but there may be some lack of clarity and/or unrelated events.	Narrative includes adequate use of details, dialogue and description.	Narrative uses adequate sensory and figurative language and/or domain-specific vocabulary.	Narrative has a few errors but is completely understandable.
2	Narrative is somewhat developed but may occasionally lose focus.	Narrative's plot is difficult to follow, and ideas are not connected well.	Narrative includes only a few details, dialogues, and descriptions.	Language in narrative is not precise or sensory; lacks domain-specific vocabulary.	Narrative has some errors in usage, grammar, spelling and/or punctuation.
1	Narrative may be confusing, unfocused, or too short.	Narrative has little or no apparent plot.	Narrative includes few or no details, dialogue or description.	Language in narrative is vague, unclear, or confusing.	Narrative is hard to follow because of frequent errors.
0	Narrative gets no credit if it does not demonstrate adequate command of narrative writing traits.				

ⓒ Common Core State Standards

Writing 3. Write narratives to develop real or imagined experiences or events using effective technique, descriptive details, and clear event sequences. **Writing 9.** Draw evidence from literary or informational texts to support analysis, reflection, and research. **Writing 9.a.** Apply grade 4 Reading standards to literature (e.g., "Describe in depth a character, setting, or event in a story or drama, drawing on specific details in the text [e.g., a character's thoughts, words, or actions]."). **Writing 9.b.** Apply grade 4 Reading standards to informational texts (e.g., "Explain how an author uses reasons and evidence to support particular points in a text").

Prove It!
Narrative Short Story

ELL

Introduce Genre Write *narrative* on the board. Explain that a narrative is a story. A short story is a fictional narrative that is meant to be read in one sitting. Explain that narratives can also be true stories. A biography is an example of a nonfiction narrative.

All in Good Time

Narrative Short Story

In this unit, students have had the opportunity to write in the narrative mode. Remind students of texts and writing tasks (such as Write Like a Reporter and Connect the Texts) in which they have encountered and practiced narrative writing.

Key Features of a Narrative Short Story

- creates a situation and introduces the narrator and characters
- organizes a sequence of events
- uses dialogue, pacing, and description to develop characters and events
- uses transitions to show sequence
- uses concrete words and sensory details to convey events
- provides a conclusion that follows from the events

Writing Task Overview

Each unit writing task provides students with an opportunity to write to sources. To successfully complete the task, students must analyze, synthesize, and evaluate multiple complex texts and create their own written response.

All in Good Time

Part 1: Students will reread and take notes on the selected sources. They will then respond to several questions about these sources and discuss their written responses with partners or in small groups.

Part 2: Students will work individually to plan, write, and revise their own short story.

Scorable Products: evidence-based short responses, narrative short story

All in Good Time: Writing Task – Short Story

Teacher Directions:

1. **Introduce the Sources** Refer students to the following texts in the Student Edition:

   1. *The Case of the Gasping Garbage,* pp. 26–41

   2. *Seeker of Knowledge,* pp. 118–129

   3. *Encyclopedia Brown and the Case of the Slippery Salamander,* pp. 146–155

   Explain to students that they will need to draw evidence and support from the texts above in order to answer evidence-based short response questions and to write a narrative short story. Students should take notes and categorize information as they closely reread the texts. Students should be given paper or a relevant graphic organizer from the TR DVD for note-taking.

2. **Provide Student Directions and Scoring Information (p. 126)** Answer any task-related questions students may have. If necessary, provide additional paper for students to write their responses.

3. **Initiate the Writing Task** If you are timing this part of the task, you may wish to alert students when half the allotted time has elapsed and again when 5 minutes remain.

4. **Facilitate Collaboration** After students have completed their written responses to the evidence-based short response questions, assign partners so that students can discuss their responses. As needed, model ways to paraphrase or restate the points a speaker makes. For example, say, "You began by saying _____. Then you made the point that ____. You used this evidence to support your point: _____."

Ⓒ **Common Core State Standards**

Writing 3. Write narratives to develop real or imagined experiences or events using effective technique, descriptive details, and clear event sequences. **Speaking/Listening 1.** Engage effectively in a range of collaborative discussions (one-on-one, in groups, and teacher-led) with diverse partners on grade 4 topics and texts, building on others' ideas and expressing their own clearly. **(Also Writing 3.a., Writing 3.b., Writing 3.c., Writing 3.d., Writing 3.e.)**

Scoring Information

Use the following 2-point scoring rubrics to evaluate students' answers to the evidence-based short response questions.

1. Compare and contrast the way the authors organize the events in their stories. Do they all tell about events in the order they happened, from first to last? Cite specific examples of time-order words or phrases.

Analysis Rubric	
2	The response: • demonstrates the ability to analyze similarities and differences in sequences of events and use of time-order words • includes specific details that make reference to the texts
1	The response: • demonstrates a limited ability to analyze similarities and differences in sequences of events and use of time-order words • includes some details that make reference to the texts
0	A response receives no credit if it demonstrates no ability to analyze similarities and differences among the texts or includes no relevant details from the texts.

2. Is the order, or sequence, of events in each source clear? Is it interesting? What specific changes would you suggest to improve the way the authors organize the events? Use details and examples from the sources.

Synthesis Rubric	
2	The response: • demonstrates the ability to synthesize information about event sequence in order to suggest improvements • includes specific details that make reference to the texts
1	The response: • demonstrates a limited ability to synthesize information about event sequence in order to suggest improvements • includes some details that make reference to the texts
0	A response receives no credit if it demonstrates no ability to synthesize information about event sequence from the sources or includes no relevant details from the texts.

3. Which of the three authors has organized the sequence of events best? Why? Include specific details and examples from the sources to support your judgment.

Evaluation Rubric	
2	The response: • demonstrates the ability to evaluate an author's organization of events in a narrative • includes specific details that make reference to the texts
1	The response: • demonstrates a limited ability to evaluate an author's organization of events in a narrative • includes some details that make reference to the texts
0	A response receives no credit if it demonstrates no ability to evaluate the use of time order or includes no relevant details from the texts.

© **Common Core State Standards**

Writing 8. Recall relevant information from experiences or gather relevant information from print and digital sources; take notes and categorize information, and provide a list of sources. **Writing 9.** Draw evidence from literary or informational texts to support analysis, reflection, and research.

All in Good Time
Writing Task – Short Response

Student Directions:

Your assignment You will reread several selections from Unit 4 and take notes on these sources. Then you will answer three questions about these materials. You may refer to your notes or to any of the sources as often as you like.

Sources

1. *The Case of the Gasping Garbage*, pp. 26–41

2. *Seeker of Knowledge*, pp. 118–129

3. *Encyclopedia Brown and the Case of the Slippery Salamander*, pp. 146–155

Be sure to read closely and take good notes. Your sources and notes will be the basis for writing your own short story in the second half of this writing task.

Evidence-Based Short Response Questions Answer the short response questions on the lines provided below each question. Your answers to these questions will be scored. Be sure to base your answers on the sources you have just read. Remember that you may refer back to your notes or to any of the sources.

After you have answered the questions, you will discuss your responses with a partner or within a small group. Your teacher will let you know when to begin the discussion part of this task.

Scoring Information Your responses will be scored based on how you demonstrate the ability to:

- compare information across texts
- include specific details and examples from the three sources
- identify, analyze, synthesize, and evaluate information from the sources
- distinguish key details from unnecessary information

Evidence-Based Short Response Questions

1. Compare and contrast the way the authors organize the events in their stories. Do they all tell about events in the order they happened, from first to last? Cite specific examples of time-order words or phrases.

_____

_____

_____

_____

2. Is the order, or sequence, of events in each source clear? Is it interesting? What specific changes would you suggest to improve the way the authors organize the events? Use details and examples from the sources.

_____

_____

_____

_____

3. Which of the three authors has organized the sequence of events best? Why? Include specific details and examples from the sources to support your judgment.

_____

_____

_____

_____

Collaborative Discussion

After you have written your responses to the questions, discuss your ideas. Your teacher will assign you a partner or a small group.

All in Good Time: Writing Task – Short Story

Teacher Directions:

1. **Provide Student Directions and Scoring Information (p. 130)** Explain to students that they will now review their notes and sources, and plan, draft, and revise their short stories. Although they may use their notes and sources, they must work alone. Students will be allowed to look back at the answers they wrote to the short response questions, but they are not allowed to make changes to those answers. Have students read the directions for the short story and answer any task-related questions they may have. Students should be given paper on which to write their short stories.

2. **Initiate the Writing Task** If you are timing this part of the task, you may wish to suggest approximate times for students to begin writing and revising. If students wish to continue writing rather than revising, allow them to do so. Alert students when 5 minutes remain.

3. **Scoring Information** Use the scoring rubric on the next page to evaluate students' short stories.

4. **Short Story Prompt** Use what you have learned from reading *The Case of the Gasping Garbage, Seeker of Knowledge,* and *Encyclopedia Brown and the Case of the Slippery Salamander* to write a short story about solving a puzzle or mystery. Organize the events in time order from beginning to end, except for one place where you look back to a past event. Refer to the texts you reread to help you decide how best to organize the events in your story.

	4-Point Narrative Writing Rubric				
Score	**Narrative Focus**	**Organization**	**Development of Narrative**	**Language and Vocabulary**	**Conventions**
4	Short story is clearly focused and developed throughout.	Short story has a well-developed, logical, easy-to-follow plot.	Short story includes thorough and effective use of details, pacing, dialogue, and description.	Short story uses precise, concrete, sensory language as well as figurative language.	Short story has correct grammar, usage, spelling, capitalization, and punctuation.
3	Short story is mostly focused and developed throughout.	Short story has a plot, but there may be some lack of clarity and/or unrelated events.	Short story includes adequate use of details, pacing, dialogue, and description.	Short story uses adequate sensory and figurative language.	Short story has a few errors in conventions but is completely understandable.
2	Short story is somewhat developed but may occasionally lose focus.	Short story's plot is difficult to follow, and ideas are not connected well.	Short story includes only a few details, dialogues, and descriptions.	Language in short story is not concrete, precise, or sensory.	Short story has some errors in usage, grammar, spelling, and/or punctuation.
1	Short story may be confusing, unfocused, or too short.	Short story has little or no apparent plot.	Short story includes few or no details, dialogue, or description.	Language in short story is vague, unclear, or confusing.	Short story is hard to follow because of frequent errors.
0	Short story gets no credit if it does not demonstrate adequate command of narrative writing traits.				

© **Common Core State Standards**

Writing 3. Write narratives to develop real or imagined experiences or events using effective technique, descriptive details, and clear event sequences. **Writing 9.** Draw evidence from literary or informational texts to support analysis, reflection, and research. **(Also Writing 3.a., Writing 3.b., Writing 3.c., Writing 10.)**

All in Good Time
Writing Task – Short Story

Student Directions:

Your Assignment Now you will review your notes and sources, and plan, draft, and revise your short story. While you may use your notes and refer to the sources, you must work on your own. You may also refer to the answers you wrote to earlier questions, but you cannot change those answers.

Short Story Prompt Use what you have learned from reading *The Case of the Gasping Garbage, Seeker of Knowledge,* and *Encyclopedia Brown and the Case of the Slippery Salamander* to write a short story about solving a puzzle or mystery. Organize the events in time order from beginning to end, except for one place where you look back to a past event. Refer to the texts you reread to help you decide how best to organize the events in your story.

Scoring Information Your short story will be assigned a score for

1. **Focus** – how well you introduce the situation and the narrator and characters

2. **Organization** – how well you arrange events in a clear and natural order, using time-order words like *before* and *later*

3. **Elaboration** – how well you use descriptive details, pacing, and dialogue to develop characters and events

4. **Language and Vocabulary** – how well you use concrete words to describe characters and events precisely

5. **Conventions** – how well you follow the rules of grammar, usage, capitalization, punctuation, and spelling

Now begin work on your short story. Try to manage your time carefully so that you can

- plan your short story

- write your short story

- revise and edit for a final draft

All in Good Time: Writing Task – Short Story

Teacher Directions:

1. Publish Explain to students that publishing their writing is the last step in the writing process. If time permits, have students review one another's stories and incorporate any comments their classmates have. Offer students suggestions for how to publish their work in an online or print magazine, and encourage them to share their work in a presentation that may include props, other visuals, and sound effects.

2. Present Students will now have the option to present their short stories. Have students give dramatic readings of their stories to the class. Use the list below to offer students some tips on listening and speaking.

While Listening to a Classmate...
- Paraphrase key story events in your notes as you listen.
- Show interest through your posture and the look on your face.

While Speaking to Classmates...
- Use different voices for different characters; use sound effects for events.
- Use props or visuals to bring actions to life.
- Speak clearly and at an understandable pace.

Things to Do Together...
- Keep your role in mind: speak to entertain, or listen to be entertained.
- Follow agreed upon rules for class presentations and discussions.
- Contribute to discussions by building on the comments of others.

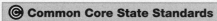 **Common Core State Standards**

Writing 6. With some guidance and support from adults, use technology, including the Internet, to produce and publish writing as well as to interact and collaborate with others; demonstrate sufficient command of keyboarding skills to type a minimum of one page in a single sitting. **Speaking/Listening 1.b.** Follow agreed-upon rules for discussions and carry out assigned roles. **Speaking/Listening 1.c.** Pose and respond to specific questions to clarify or follow up on information, and make comments that contribute to the discussion and link to the remarks of others. **Speaking/Listening 2.** Paraphrase portions of a text read aloud or information presented in diverse media and formats, including visually, quantitatively, and orally. **Speaking/Listening 5.** Add audio recordings and visual displays to presentations when appropriate to enhance the development of main ideas or themes.

Unit 5 Adventures by Land, Air, and Water

Writing Focus: Argument

Write Like a Reporter
Argumentative Paragraph

Student Prompt Reread *Smokejumpers*. In your opinion, why must smokejumpers think of their own safety first? Write a paragraph clearly stating your opinion and giving reasons for it that you support with evidence from the text. Describe a danger smokejumpers face. Choose supporting details from information about equipment (pp. 184–185), jumping (pp. 186–189), or returning home (p. 190). Make sure to link your opinion and reasons using words and phrases such as *for instance, in order to,* and *in addition*.

_____

_____

_____

_____

_____

_____

_____

_____

_____

_____

_____

_____

_____

Write Like a Reporter
Argumentative Paragraph

> **Student Prompt, p. 134** Reread *Smokejumpers*. In your opinion, why must smokejumpers think of their own safety first? Write a paragraph clearly stating your opinion and giving reasons for it that you support with evidence from the text. Describe a danger smokejumpers face. Choose supporting details from information about equipment (pp. 184–185), jumping (pp. 186–189), or returning home (p. 190). Make sure to link your opinion and reasons using words and phrases such as *for instance, in order to,* and *in addition*.

Writing to Sources After students reread *Smokejumpers,* discuss the dangers the firefighters face not only from fire, but also from jumping out of planes. Have students write introductory sentences that state their opinions. Then guide them to work closely with one part of the text to select evidence that will support their opinions. Advise students to arrange the details in a logical progression and use transitional strategies to link them with their opinions.

Students' paragraphs should:

- clearly state an opinion
- provide reasons that are supported by details
- link opinion and reasons using words and phrases
- demonstrate strong command of the conventions of standard written English

Ⓒ **Common Core State Standards**

Writing 1. Write opinion pieces on topics or texts, supporting a point of view with reasons and information. **Writing 9.** Draw evidence from literary or informational texts to support analysis, reflection, and research. **Writing 9.b.** Apply grade 4 Reading standards to informational texts (e.g., "Explain how an author uses reasons and evidence to support particular points in a text").

Connect the Texts
Argumentative Paragraph

Student Prompt Review *Smokejumpers* and "Camp With Care." Both support the idea that people should protect nature. Why is protecting nature a good thing to do? State your answer to that question as an opinion. In a one-paragraph argument, use facts from both texts as reasons for your opinion. Write in a logical sequence so you can finish with a strong concluding sentence that restates your opinion.

_____

_____

_____

_____

_____

_____

_____

_____

_____

_____

_____

_____

_____

_____

Connect the Texts
Argumentative Paragraph

Student Prompt, p. 136 Review *Smokejumpers* and "Camp With Care." Both support the idea that people should protect nature. Why is protecting nature a good thing to do? State your answer to that question as an opinion. In a one-paragraph argument, use facts from both texts as reasons for your opinion. Write in a logical sequence so you can finish with a strong concluding sentence that restates your opinion.

Writing to Sources Ask students if they agree that people should protect nature. Guide them as they prepare to write an argument that supports their answer. Have them reread *Smokejumpers* and "Camp With Care," making a list of facts that support their opinion. Tell students to organize their facts in a logical sequence before they write their paragraphs. Remind them to include a final sentence that restates their opinions convincingly.

	4-point Argument Writing Rubric				
Score	**Statement of Purpose/Focus**	**Organization**	**Development of Evidence**	**Language and Vocabulary**	**Conventions**
4	Opinion is clearly conveyed and well supported; response is focused.	Organization is clear and effective, creating a sense of cohesion.	Evidence is thorough and persuasive, and includes facts and details.	Ideas are clearly and effectively conveyed, using precise language and/or domain-specific vocabulary.	Command of conventions is strongly demonstrated.
3	Opinion is clear, adequately supported; response is generally focused.	Organization is clear, though minor flaws may be present and some ideas may be disconnected.	Evidence is adequate and includes facts and details.	Ideas are adequately conveyed, using both precise and more general language; may include domain-specific vocabulary.	Command of conventions is sufficiently demonstrated.
2	Opinion is somewhat supported; response may lack focus or include unnecessary material.	Organization is inconsistent, and flaws are apparent.	Evidence is uneven or incomplete; insufficient use of facts and details.	Ideas are unevenly conveyed, using overly-simplistic language; lack of domain-specific vocabulary.	Command of conventions is uneven.
1	The response may be confusing, unfocused; opinion not sufficiently supported.	Organization is poor or nonexistent.	Evidence is poor or nonexistent.	Ideas are conveyed in a vague, unclear, or confusing manner.	There is very little command of conventions.
0	The response shows no evidence of the ability to construct a coherent opinion essay using information from sources.				

Ⓒ Common Core State Standards

Writing 1. Write opinion pieces on topics or texts, supporting a point of view with reasons and information. **Writing 9.** Draw evidence from literary or informational texts to support analysis, reflection, and research. **Writing 9.b.** Apply grade 4 Reading standards to informational texts (e.g., "Explain how an author uses reasons and evidence to support particular points in a text").

Write Like a Reporter
Argumentative Paragraph

Student Prompt Reread *Lost City*. Pay attention to the Quechua boy and Hiram Bingham. In your opinion, who was more excited about the discovery? Why? Write a one-paragraph argument based on your opinion. First introduce your topic and the feelings of the two characters. Then say who was more excited. Give at least two reasons based on details in the biography. Link the reasons to your opinion using transitional words or phrases.

_____

_____

_____

_____

_____

_____

_____

_____

_____

_____

_____

_____

_____

_____

_____

_____

Write Like a Reporter
Argumentative Paragraph

Student Prompt, p. 138 Reread *Lost City.* Pay attention to the Quechua boy and Hiram Bingham. In your opinion, who was more excited about the discovery? Why? Write a one-paragraph argument based on your opinion. First introduce your topic and the feelings of the two characters. Then say who was more excited. Give at least two reasons based on details in the biography. Link the reasons to your opinion using transitional words or phrases.

Writing to Sources After they reread the biography, have students explain the background each character brought to the discovery. Ask how they know that each one felt excited. Then have them prepare their argument paragraphs. Explain that the first sentence should clearly state the topic or opinion. Remind students to use details from the biography as the reasons they give for their opinions. Tell them they must link their reasons to their opinions with transitional words or phrases.

Students' paragraphs should:

- clearly introduce a topic
- provide reasons that are supported by details
- link opinions and reasons using words and phrases
- demonstrate strong command of the conventions of standard written English

---

ⓒ Common Core State Standards

Writing 1. Write opinion pieces on topics or texts, supporting a point of view with reasons and information. **Writing 9.** Draw evidence from literary or informational texts to support analysis, reflection, and research. **Writing 9.b.** Apply grade 4 Reading standards to informational texts (e.g., "Explain how an author uses reasons and evidence to support particular points in a text").

Connect the Texts
Argumentative Paragraph

> **Student Prompt** Reread "Riding the Rails to Machu Picchu," especially the introduction of three ways to visit the site on p. 223. Then review *Lost City*. Based on both readings, choose the best way to go to Machu Picchu. Write a paragraph stating your opinion. Clearly state your opinion at the beginning and give reasons for your opinion using details from both readings. Finally, conclude your paragraph with a sentence that sums up your opinion and your reasoning.

_____

_____

_____

_____

_____

_____

_____

_____

_____

_____

_____

_____

_____

Connect the Texts
Argumentative Paragraph

Student Prompt, p. 140 Reread "Riding the Rails to Machu Picchu," especially the introduction of three ways to visit the site on p. 223. Then review *Lost City*. Based on both readings, choose the best way to go to Machu Picchu. Write a paragraph stating your opinion. Clearly state your opinion at the beginning and give reasons for your opinion using details from both readings. Finally, conclude your paragraph with a sentence that sums up your opinion and your reasoning.

Writing to Sources Have students list the three ways to get to Machu Picchu (hike, helicopter, train). Invite them to think about the descriptions in the readings. Have students choose how to get to the site and begin their argument paragraphs by stating their choices. Remind them to use details from both readings in the reasons they give to support their opinions.

	4-point Argument Writing Rubric				
Score	Statement of Purpose/Focus	Organization	Development of Evidence	Language and Vocabulary	Conventions
4	Opinion is clearly conveyed and well supported; response is focused.	Organization is clear and effective, creating a sense of cohesion.	Evidence is thorough and persuasive, and includes facts and details.	Ideas are clearly and effectively conveyed, using precise language and/or domain-specific vocabulary.	Command of conventions is strongly demonstrated.
3	Opinion is clear, adequately supported; response is generally focused.	Organization is clear, though minor flaws may be present and some ideas may be disconnected.	Evidence is adequate and includes facts and details.	Ideas are adequately conveyed, using both precise and more general language; may include domain-specific vocabulary.	Command of conventions is sufficiently demonstrated.
2	Opinion is somewhat supported; response may lack focus or include unnecessary material.	Organization is inconsistent, and flaws are apparent.	Evidence is uneven or incomplete; insufficient use of facts and details.	Ideas are unevenly conveyed, using overly-simplistic language; lack of domain-specific vocabulary.	Command of conventions is uneven.
1	The response may be confusing, unfocused; opinion not sufficiently supported.	Organization is poor or nonexistent.	Evidence is poor or nonexistent.	Ideas are conveyed in a vague, unclear, or confusing manner.	There is very little command of conventions.
0	The response shows no evidence of the ability to construct a coherent opinion essay using information from sources.				

© Common Core State Standards

Writing 1. Write opinion pieces on topics or texts, supporting a point of view with reasons and information. **Writing 9.** Draw evidence from literary or informational texts to support analysis, reflection, and research. **Writing 9.b.** Apply grade 4 Reading standards to informational texts (e.g., "Explain how an author uses reasons and evidence to support particular points in a text").

Name _____

Write Like a Reporter
Argumentative Paragraph

Student Prompt Reread *Cliff Hanger*. Think about whether it was okay for Axel to take the risk of climbing in a storm. Write a one-paragraph argument in which you clearly state your opinion and give facts from the story to support it. The description of how Axel makes the climb on pp. 239–243 is an especially good source of facts. Use linking words and phrases to organize your argument.

_____

_____

_____

_____

_____

_____

_____

_____

_____

_____

_____

_____

_____

_____

Write Like a Reporter

Argumentative Paragraph

> **Student Prompt, p. 142** Reread *Cliff Hanger.* Think about whether it was okay for Axel to take the risk of climbing in a storm. Write a one-paragraph argument in which you clearly state your opinion and give facts from the story to support it. The description of how Axel makes the climb on pp. 239–243 is an especially good source of facts. Use linking words and phrases to organize your argument.

Writing to Sources After students reread the story, ask them why they think Dag helped Axel climb to save his dog. Tell students to look in the story for details about Axel's climb that might explain Dag's confidence in his son. Then direct students to write one-paragraph arguments giving their opinions and supporting them with reasons based on facts from the story. Tell students to give examples of the skills and equipment Axel mastered using vocabulary from the reading.

Students' paragraphs should:

- state an opinion
- provide reasons that are supported by facts
- use words and phrases that link reasons to the opinion
- demonstrate strong command of the conventions of standard written English

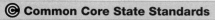 **Common Core State Standards**

Writing 1. Write opinion pieces on topics or texts, supporting a point of view with reasons and information. **Writing 9.** Draw evidence from literary or informational texts to support analysis, reflection, and research. **Writing 9.a.** Apply grade 4 Reading standards to literature (e.g., "Describe in depth a character, setting, or event in a story or drama, drawing on specific details in the text [e.g., a character's thoughts, words, or actions].").

Connect the Texts
Argumentative Paragraph

Student Prompt Reread *Cliff Hanger* and "Rock Climbing." Do you agree or disagree with the following statement: Conducting Internet research on different types of rock formations helps climbers know what to expect when they climb. State your opinion in a one-paragraph argument that you support with reasoning from both passages. Make sure to organize your reasons in a logical order.

_____

_____

_____

_____

_____

_____

_____

_____

_____

_____

_____

_____

_____

_____

_____

_____

Connect the Texts
Argumentative Paragraph

> **Student Prompt, p. 144** Reread *Cliff Hanger* and "Rock Climbing." Do you agree or disagree with the following statement: Conducting Internet research on different types of rock formations helps climbers know what to expect when they climb. State your opinion in a one-paragraph argument that you support with reasoning from both passages. Make sure to organize your reasons in a logical order.

Writing to Sources Discuss with students the benefit of research before participating in an activity. Ask students to agree or disagree with the statement. Then ask students to write one-paragraph arguments in which they defend their opinions with reasoning from the texts. Students should organize their arguments using concrete details and draw conclusions from both passages.

4-point Argument Writing Rubric					
Score	**Statement of Purpose/Focus**	**Organization**	**Development of Evidence**	**Language and Vocabulary**	**Conventions**
4	Opinion is clearly conveyed and well supported; response is focused.	Organization is clear and effective, creating a sense of cohesion.	Evidence is thorough and persuasive, and includes facts and details.	Ideas are clearly and effectively conveyed, using precise language and/or domain-specific vocabulary.	Command of conventions is strongly demonstrated.
3	Opinion is clear, adequately supported; response is generally focused.	Organization is clear, though minor flaws may be present and some ideas may be disconnected.	Evidence is adequate and includes facts and details.	Ideas are adequately conveyed, using both precise and more general language; may include domain-specific vocabulary.	Command of conventions is sufficiently demonstrated.
2	Opinion is somewhat supported; response may lack focus or include unnecessary material.	Organization is inconsistent, and flaws are apparent.	Evidence is uneven or incomplete; insufficient use of facts and details.	Ideas are unevenly conveyed, using overly-simplistic language; lack of domain-specific vocabulary.	Command of conventions is uneven.
1	The response may be confusing, unfocused; opinion not sufficiently supported.	Organization is poor or nonexistent.	Evidence is poor or nonexistent.	Ideas are conveyed in a vague, unclear, or confusing manner.	There is very little command of conventions.
0	The response shows no evidence of the ability to construct a coherent opinion essay using information from sources.				

ⓒ Common Core State Standards

Writing 1. Write opinion pieces on topics or texts, supporting a point of view with reasons and information. **Writing 9.** Draw evidence from literary or informational texts to support analysis, reflection, and research. **Writing 9.a.** Apply grade 4 Reading standards to literature (e.g., "Describe in depth a character, setting, or event in a story or drama, drawing on specific details in the text [e.g., a character's thoughts, words, or actions]."). **Writing 9.b.** Apply grade 4 Reading standards to informational texts (e.g., "Explain how an author uses reasons and evidence to support particular points in a text").

Write Like a Reporter
Argumentative Paragraph

Student Prompt Reread *Antarctic Journal*. Think about the letters the author writes to her loved ones as well as the journal entries. Was exploring the Antarctic a good thing for the author to do? What were the risks and rewards? Write a paragraph stating your opinion. Give reasons that you support with details from the text. Connect your opinion and reasons using linking words and phrases.

_____

_____

_____

_____

_____

_____

_____

_____

_____

_____

_____

_____

_____

_____

_____

_____

Write Like a Reporter
Argumentative Paragraph

Student Prompt, p. 146 Reread *Antarctic Journal.* Think about the letters the author writes to her loved ones as well as the journal entries. Was exploring the Antarctic a good thing for the author to do? What were the risks and rewards? Write a paragraph stating your opinion. Give reasons that you support with details from the text. Connect your opinion and reasons using linking words and phrases.

Writing to Sources As students reread *Antarctic Journal,* have them list two exciting experiences they would like to have themselves. Invite them to imagine what it was like to receive the author's letters. Then have students write one-paragraph arguments that state their opinions, give reasons, and use details from the journal and the letters to support their reasons. Suggest linking words and phrases, such as *because, for example,* and *therefore,* that they can use to connect their reasons and opinions.

Students' paragraphs should:

- clearly state an opinion
- provide reasons that are supported by details
- link opinion and reasons using words and phrases
- demonstrate strong command of the conventions of standard written English

Ⓒ **Common Core State Standards**

Writing 1. Write opinion pieces on topics or texts, supporting a point of view with reasons and information. **Writing 9.** Draw evidence from literary or informational texts to support analysis, reflection, and research. **Writing 9.b.** Apply grade 4 Reading standards to informational texts (e.g., "Explain how an author uses reasons and evidence to support particular points in a text").

Connect the Texts
Argumentative Paragraph

> **Student Prompt** Reread *Antarctic Journal* and "Swimming Towards Ice."
> Identify the dangers the women faced, such as freezing cold and falling into
> a crevasse. Then answer the question: Are the rewards worth the risk? In
> one paragraph, give reasons to support your opinion using details from the
> reading. Create an organizational structure that groups related details. Finish
> with a concluding statement related to your opinion.

_____

_____

_____

_____

_____

_____

_____

_____

_____

_____

_____

_____

_____

_____

Connect the Texts
Argumentative Paragraph

Student Prompt, p. 148 Reread *Antarctic Journal* and "Swimming Towards Ice." Identify the dangers the women faced, such as freezing cold and falling into a crevasse. Then answer the question: Are the rewards worth the risk? In one paragraph, give reasons to support your opinion using details from the reading. Create an organizational structure that groups related details. Finish with a concluding statement related to your opinion.

Writing to Sources Ask students what the women in the texts have in common. Discuss with students their opinions about the rewards each woman gets from her experiences. Then have them find specific details in each reading to support their opinions. Tell them to create organized paragraphs using the details and finishing with concluding statements.

4-point Argument Writing Rubric					
Score	Statement of Purpose/Focus	Organization	Development of Evidence	Language and Vocabulary	Conventions
4	Opinion is clearly conveyed and well supported; response is focused.	Organization is clear and effective, creating a sense of cohesion.	Evidence is thorough and persuasive, and includes facts and details.	Ideas are clearly and effectively conveyed, using precise language and/or domain-specific vocabulary.	Command of conventions is strongly demonstrated.
3	Opinion is clear, adequately supported; response is generally focused.	Organization is clear, though minor flaws may be present and some ideas may be disconnected.	Evidence is adequate and includes facts and details.	Ideas are adequately conveyed, using both precise and more general language; may include domain-specific vocabulary.	Command of conventions is sufficiently demonstrated.
2	Opinion is somewhat supported; response may lack focus or include unnecessary material.	Organization is inconsistent, and flaws are apparent.	Evidence is uneven or incomplete; insufficient use of facts and details.	Ideas are unevenly conveyed, using overly-simplistic language; lack of domain-specific vocabulary.	Command of conventions is uneven.
1	The response may be confusing, unfocused; opinion not sufficiently supported.	Organization is poor or nonexistent.	Evidence is poor or nonexistent.	Ideas are conveyed in a vague, unclear, or confusing manner.	There is very little command of conventions.
0	The response shows no evidence of the ability to construct a coherent opinion essay using information from sources.				

ⓒ Common Core State Standards

Writing 1. Write opinion pieces on topics or texts, supporting a point of view with reasons and information. **Writing 9.** Draw evidence from literary or informational texts to support analysis, reflection, and research. **Writing 9.b.** Apply grade 4 Reading standards to informational texts (e.g., "Explain how an author uses reasons and evidence to support particular points in a text").

Write Like a Reporter
Argumentative Paragraph

Student Prompt Reread the story, and then look at p. 304, when the brothers are safe in the shelter. Gerry has mixed feelings when he realizes his dad is not back yet. Do you think he should be glad or sorry? Clearly state your opinion in a paragraph. Give reasons that you support with details from the story. Conclude your paragraph with a statement related to your opinion.

_____

_____

_____

_____

_____

_____

_____

_____

_____

_____

_____

_____

_____

_____

_____

_____

_____

Write Like a Reporter
Argumentative Paragraph

Student Prompt, p. 150 Reread the story, and then look at p. 304, when the brothers are safe in the shelter. Gerry has mixed feelings when he realizes his dad is not back yet. Do you think he should be glad or sorry? Clearly state your opinion in a paragraph. Give reasons that you support with details from the story. Conclude your paragraph with a statement related to your opinion.

Writing to Sources After students reread the story, have them think about how the brothers relate to each other and to their father. Ask why Gerry has mixed emotions when they get to the shelter. Have students choose which emotion they think he should feel. Tell them that their paragraphs should clearly state their opinions and reasons. Explain that they must use details from the story to support their reasons. Finally, tell them to write a concluding sentence related to their opinions.

Students' paragraphs should:

- clearly state an opinion
- provide reasons that are supported by details
- provide a concluding sentence related to the opinion presented
- demonstrate strong command of the conventions of standard written English

© Common Core State Standards

Writing 1. Write opinion pieces on topics or texts, supporting a point of view with reasons and information. **Writing 9.** Draw evidence from literary or informational texts to support analysis, reflection, and research. **Writing 9.a.** Apply grade 4 Reading standards to literature (e.g., "Describe in depth a character, setting, or event in a story or drama, drawing on specific details in the text [e.g., a character's thoughts, words, or actions].").

Connect the Texts
Argumentative Paragraph

Student Prompt Reread *Moonwalk* and "A Walk on the Moon." Pay attention to facts about the moon in the story and in the article. Does the author of *Moonwalk* contribute to or distract from the story by including so many facts about the moon? What other facts from "A Walk on the Moon" would add to the story of *Moonwalk*? Give your opinion and explain your reasons in a paragraph. Support your reasons with facts from both texts. Connect your opinion and your reasons with linking words and phrases.

_____

_____

_____

_____

_____

_____

_____

_____

_____

_____

_____

_____

_____

Connect the Texts
Argumentative Paragraph

Student Prompt, p. 152 Reread *Moonwalk* and "A Walk on the Moon." Pay attention to facts about the moon in the story and in the article. Does the author of *Moonwalk* contribute to or distract from the story by including so many facts about the moon? What other facts from "A Walk on the Moon" would add to the story of *Moonwalk*? Give your opinion and explain your reasons in a paragraph. Support your reasons with facts from both texts. Connect your opinion and your reasons with linking words and phrases.

Writing to Sources After they reread the texts, remind students that the first moonwalk took place a long time ago. Ask students to discuss the author's choice to set the story of *Moonwalk* on the moon and what the inclusion of facts adds to the story. Students should include facts and details from both passages in their arguments. Remind them to clearly state an opinion and to link their reasons and opinion using words and phrases.

4-point Argument Writing Rubric					
Score	Statement of Purpose/Focus	Organization	Development of Evidence	Language and Vocabulary	Conventions
4	Opinion is clearly conveyed and well supported; response is focused.	Organization is clear and effective, creating a sense of cohesion.	Evidence is thorough and persuasive, and includes facts and details.	Ideas are clearly and effectively conveyed, using precise language and/or domain-specific vocabulary.	Command of conventions is strongly demonstrated.
3	Opinion is clear, adequately supported; response is generally focused.	Organization is clear, though minor flaws may be present and some ideas may be disconnected.	Evidence is adequate and includes facts and details.	Ideas are adequately conveyed, using both precise and more general language; may include domain-specific vocabulary.	Command of conventions is sufficiently demonstrated.
2	Opinion is somewhat supported; response may lack focus or include unnecessary material.	Organization is inconsistent, and flaws are apparent.	Evidence is uneven or incomplete; insufficient use of facts and details.	Ideas are unevenly conveyed, using overly-simplistic language; lack of domain-specific vocabulary.	Command of conventions is uneven.
1	The response may be confusing, unfocused; opinion not sufficiently supported.	Organization is poor or nonexistent.	Evidence is poor or nonexistent.	Ideas are conveyed in a vague, unclear, or confusing manner.	There is very little command of conventions.
0	The response shows no evidence of the ability to construct a coherent opinion essay using information from sources.				

© Common Core State Standards

Writing 1. Write opinion pieces on topics or texts, supporting a point of view with reasons and information. **Writing 9.** Draw evidence from literary or informational texts to support analysis, reflection, and research. **Writing 9.a.** Apply grade 4 Reading standards to literature (e.g., "Describe in depth a character, setting, or event in a story or drama, drawing on specific details in the text [e.g., a character's thoughts, words, or actions]."). **Writing 9.b.** Apply grade 4 Reading standards to informational texts (e.g., "Explain how an author uses reasons and evidence to support particular points in a text").

Prove It!
Argumentative Essay

Academic Vocabulary

In an **argumentative essay**, a writer presents an opinion and supports it with reasons and evidence. An argument tries to persuade an audience to think or act a certain way.

ELL

Introduce Genre Write *argument* on the board. Explain that an argument is a kind of persuasive writing in which a writer states his or her opinion on a topic and tries to make the reader accept it.

Adventures and Heroes

Argumentative Essay

In this unit, students have had the opportunity to write in the argument mode. Remind students of texts and writing tasks (such as Write Like a Reporter and Connect the Texts) in which they have encountered and practiced argumentative writing.

Key Features of an Argumentative Essay

- introduces a topic and states an opinion clearly
- organizes related ideas clearly
- includes reasons supported by facts and details
- includes words and phrases to link reasons to opinion
- has a conclusion related to the opinion presented

Writing Task Overview

Each unit writing task provides students with an opportunity to write to sources. To successfully complete the task, students must analyze, synthesize, and evaluate multiple complex texts and create their own written response.

Adventures and Heroes

Part 1: Students will reread and take notes on the selected sources. They will then respond to several questions about these sources and discuss their written responses with partners or in small groups.

Part 2: Students will work individually to plan, write, and revise their own argumentative essay.

Scorable Products: evidence-based short responses, argumentative essay

Adventures and Heroes: Writing Task – Short Response

Teacher Directions:

1. **Introduce the Sources** Refer students to the following texts in the Student Edition:

   1. *Smokejumpers,* pp. 178–191

   2. *Lost City,* pp. 206–217

   3. *Cliff Hanger,* pp. 234–245

   Explain to students that they will need to draw evidence and support from the texts above in order to answer evidence-based short response questions and to write an argumentative essay. Students should take notes and categorize information as they closely reread the texts. Students should be given paper or a relevant graphic organizer from the TR DVD for note-taking.

2. **Provide Student Directions and Scoring Information (p. 158)** Answer any task-related questions students may have. If necessary, provide additional paper for students to write their responses.

3. **Initiate the Writing Task** If you are timing this part of the task, you may wish to alert students when half the allotted time has elapsed and again when 5 minutes remain.

4. **Facilitate Collaboration** After students have completed their written responses to the evidence-based short response questions, assign students to small groups to discuss their responses. As needed, provide rules and strategies for students to express ideas as well as to link to and build on those of their classmates.

Ⓒ Common Core State Standards

Writing 1. Write opinion pieces on topics or texts, supporting a point of view with reasons and information. **Speaking/Listening 1.** Engage effectively in a range of collaborative discussions (one-on-one, in groups, and teacher-led) with diverse partners on *grade 4 topics and texts*, building on others' ideas and expressing their own clearly. **(Also Writing 1.a., Writing 1.b., Writing 1.c., Writing 1.d.)**

Scoring Information

Use the following 2-point scoring rubrics to evaluate students' answers to the evidence-based short response questions.

1. A smokejumper, Professor Bingham, and Axel all face dangers. Explain how each was prepared to take on those dangers. Use details from all three texts in your answer.

	Analysis Rubric	
2	The response: • demonstrates the ability to analyze similarities and differences among the texts • includes specific details that make reference to the texts	
1	The response: • demonstrates a limited ability to analyze similarities and differences among the texts • includes some details that make reference to the texts	
0	A response receives no credit if it demonstrates no ability to analyze similarities and differences among the texts or includes no relevant details from the texts.	

2. What do you imagine the smokejumpers, the professor, and the boy were most concerned about while facing their tough challenges? Contrast what you think they had on their minds during their adventures. Explain your answer using key words and phrases from the texts.

	Synthesis Rubric	
2	The response: • demonstrates the ability to synthesize information from the sources in order to contrast characters' thoughts • includes specific details that make reference to the texts	
1	The response: • demonstrates a limited ability to synthesize information from the sources in order to contrast characters' thoughts • includes some details that make reference to the texts	
0	A response receives no credit if it demonstrates no ability to synthesize or contrast information from the sources or includes no relevant details from the texts.	

3. Think about the qualities a hero possesses. Evaluate the actions of the smokejumpers, Professor Bingham, and Axel. Who is most heroic? Why? Use details from each text to support your opinion.

	Evaluation Rubric	
2	The response: • demonstrates the ability to evaluate characters as heroes • includes specific details that make reference to the texts	
1	The response: • demonstrates a limited ability to evaluate characters as heroes • includes some details that make reference to the texts	
0	A response receives no credit if it demonstrates no ability to evaluate information from the sources or includes no relevant details from the texts.	

© **Common Core State Standards**

Writing 8. Recall relevant information from experiences or gather relevant information from print and digital sources; take notes and categorize information, and provide a list of sources. **Writing 9.** Draw evidence from literary or informational texts to support analysis, reflection, and research.

Adventures and Heroes
Writing Task – Short Response

Student Directions:

Your assignment You will reread several selections from Unit 5 and take notes on these sources. Then you will answer three questions about these materials. You may refer to your notes or to any of the sources as often as you like.

Sources

1. *Smokejumpers,* pp. 178–191

2. *Lost City,* pp. 206–217

3. *Cliff Hanger,* pp. 234–245

Be sure to read closely and take good notes. Your sources and notes will be the basis for writing your own argumentative essay in the second half of this writing task.

Evidence-Based Short Response Questions Answer the short response questions on the lines provided below each question. Your answers to these questions will be scored. Be sure to base your answers on the sources you have just read. Remember that you may refer back to your notes or to any of the sources.

After you have answered the questions, you will discuss your responses with a partner or within a small group. Your teacher will let you know when to begin the discussion part of this task.

Scoring Information Your responses will be scored based on how you demonstrate the ability to:

- compare information across texts
- include relevant evidence from sources
- identify, analyze, synthesize, and evaluate information from sources
- distinguish key details and support from irrelevant information

Evidence-Based Short Response Questions

1. A smokejumper, Professor Bingham, and Axel all face dangers. Explain how each was prepared to take on those dangers. Use details from all three texts in your answer.

_____

_____

_____

_____

2. What do you imagine the smokejumpers, the professor, and the boy were most concerned about while facing their tough challenges? Contrast what you think they had on their minds during their adventures. Explain your answer using key words and phrases from the texts.

_____

_____

_____

_____

3. Think about the qualities a hero possesses. Evaluate the actions of the smokejumpers, Professor Bingham, and Axel. Who is most heroic? Why? Use details from each text to support your opinion.

_____

_____

_____

_____

Collaborative Discussion

After you have written your responses to the questions, discuss your ideas. Your teacher will assign you a partner or a small group and let you know when to begin.

Adventures and Heroes: Writing Task – Argumentative Essay

Teacher Directions:

1. **Provide Student Directions and Scoring Information (p. 162)** Explain to students that they will now review their notes and sources, and plan, draft, and revise their argumentative essays. Although they may use their notes and sources, they must work alone. Students will be allowed to look back at the answers they wrote for the short response questions, but they are not allowed to make changes to those answers. Have students read the directions for the argumentative essay and answer any task-related questions they may have. Students should be given paper on which to write their argumentative essays.

2. **Initiate the Writing Task** If you are timing this part of the task, you may wish to suggest approximate times for students to begin writing and revising. If students wish to continue writing rather than revising, allow them to do so. Alert students when 5 minutes remain.

3. **Scoring Information** Use the scoring rubric on the next page to evaluate students' argumentative essays.

4. **Argumentative Essay Prompt** The smokejumpers, Professor Bingham, and Axel all had adventures. What makes an outing or trip an adventure? Use what you have learned from reading *Smokejumpers, Lost City,* and *Cliff Hanger* to write an argumentative essay in which you state your opinion about what adventures are. Explain your reasons, supporting your opinion with details from the three texts.

4-Point Argument Writing Rubric

Score	Statement of Purpose/ Focus	Organization	Development of Evidence	Language and Vocabulary	Conventions
4	Opinion is clearly conveyed and well supported; argument is focused.	Organization is clear and effective, creating a sense of cohesion.	Evidence is thorough and persuasive, and includes facts and details.	Ideas are clearly and effectively conveyed, using precise language and/or domain-specific vocabulary.	Command of conventions is strongly demonstrated.
3	Opinion is clear and adequately supported; argument is generally focused.	Organization is clear, though minor flaws may be present and some ideas may be disconnected.	Evidence is adequate and includes facts and details.	Ideas are adequately conveyed, using both precise and more general language; may include domain-specific vocabulary.	Command of conventions is sufficiently demonstrated.
2	Opinion is somewhat supported; lacks focus or includes unnecessary material.	Organization is inconsistent and flaws are apparent.	Evidence is uneven or incomplete; insufficient use of facts and details.	Ideas are unevenly conveyed, using overly-simplistic language; lacks domain-specific vocabulary.	Command of conventions is uneven.
1	Argument may be confusing, unfocused; opinion not sufficiently supported.	Organization is poor or nonexistent.	Evidence is poor or nonexistent.	Ideas are conveyed in a vague, unclear, or confusing manner.	There is very little command of conventions.
0	The response shows no evidence of the ability to construct a coherent argumentative essay using information from sources.				

© Common Core State Standards

Writing 1. Write opinion pieces on topics or texts, supporting a point of view with reasons and information. **Writing 9.** Draw evidence from literary or informational texts to support analysis, reflection, and research. **(Also Writing 1.a., Writing 1.b., Writing 10.)**

Adventures and Heroes
Writing Task – Argumentative Essay

Student Directions:

Your Assignment Now you will review your notes and sources, and plan, draft, and revise your argumentative essay. While you may use your notes and refer to the sources, you must work on your own. You may also refer to the answers you wrote to earlier questions, but you cannot change those answers.

Argumentative Essay Prompt The smokejumpers, Professor Bingham, and Axel all had adventures. What makes an outing or trip an adventure? Use what you have learned from reading *Smokejumpers, Lost City,* and *Cliff Hanger* to write an argumentative essay in which you state your opinion about what adventures are. Explain your reasons, supporting your opinion with details from the three texts.

Scoring Information Your argumentative essay will be assigned a score for

1. **Focus** – how clearly you introduce your topic and state your opinion
2. **Organization** – how well your essay groups related ideas together, linking your opinion and reasons
3. **Elaboration** – how well you provide sound reasoning supported by specific details
4. **Language and Vocabulary** – how well you link ideas and use precise language
5. **Conventions** – how well you follow the rules of usage, punctuation, capitalization, and spelling

Now begin work on your argumentative essay. Try to manage your time carefully so that you can

- plan your argumentative essay
- write your argumentative essay
- revise and edit for a final draft

Adventures and Heroes: Writing Task – Argumentative Essay

Teacher Directions:

1. **Publish** Explain to students that publishing their writing is the last step in the writing process. If time permits, have students review one another's compositions and discuss any comments their classmates have. Offer students suggestions for how to publish their work, such as in a school newspaper, wiki, or blog post. Encourage students to use the Internet to share their work with others.

2. **Present** Have students present their argumentative essays to the class. Use the list below to offer students some tips on listening and speaking.

While Listening to a Classmate...

- Face the speaker to listen attentively.
- Identify the speaker's key ideas.
- Take notes on the reasons and evidence the speaker gives.

While Speaking to Classmates...

- Have good posture and eye contact.
- Explain your opinion and reasons in an organized way.
- Speak clearly at an appropriate pace.

Things to Do Together...

- Ask and answer questions with detail.
- Clarify or follow up on information presented.
- Contribute to the discussion and expand on each other's ideas.

Ⓒ Common Core State Standards

Writing 6. With some guidance and support from adults, use technology, including the Internet, to produce and publish writing as well as to interact and collaborate with others; demonstrate sufficient command of keyboarding skills to type a minimum of one page in a single sitting. **Speaking/ Listening 1.c.** Pose and respond to specific questions to clarify or follow up on information, and make comments that contribute to the discussion and link to the remarks of others. **Speaking/Listening 1.d.** Review the key ideas expressed and explain their own ideas and understanding in light of the discussion. **Speaking/Listening 3.** Identify the reasons and evidence a speaker provides to support particular points. **Speaking/Listening 4.** Report on a topic or text, tell a story, or recount an experience in an organized manner, using appropriate facts and relevant, descriptive details to support main ideas or themes; speak clearly at an understandable pace.

Unit 6 Reaching for Goals

Writing Focus: Informative/Explanatory

Write Like a Reporter
Informative/Explanatory Paragraph

Student Prompt Write a summary of the section in *My Brother Martin* that describes the children's experiences on Auburn Avenue. Begin with a general observation, and then focus on one or two experiences that mean the most. In precise language, give concrete details to describe the experiences. Use examples from the text to develop your summary paragraph.

_____

_____

_____

_____

_____

_____

_____

_____

_____

_____

_____

_____

_____

_____

_____

_____

Write Like a Reporter
Informative/Explanatory Paragraph

Student Prompt, p. 166 Write a summary of the section in *My Brother Martin* that describes the children's experiences on Auburn Avenue. Begin with a general observation, and then focus on one or two experiences that mean the most. In precise language, give concrete details to describe the experiences. Use examples from the text to develop your summary paragraph.

Writing to Sources After students reread the biography, have them summarize the main neighborhood events that take place on Auburn Avenue. Encourage them to begin their one-paragraph summary with a general statement about the significance of the experiences. Then have them focus on the most meaningful experiences. Remind them to use concrete details, precise language, and examples from the text to develop the topic.

Students' paragraphs should:

- provide a general observation and a focus
- develop the topic with concrete details and examples from the text
- use precise language to convey information
- demonstrate strong command of the conventions of standard written English

© Common Core State Standards

Writing 2. Write informative/explanatory texts to examine a topic and convey ideas and information clearly. **Writing 9.** Draw evidence from literary or informational texts to support analysis, reflection, and research. **Writing 9.b.** Apply grade 4 Reading standards to informational texts (e.g., "Explain how an author uses reasons and evidence to support particular points in a text").

Connect the Texts
Informative/Explanatory Summary

> **Student Prompt** Summarize the way metaphors and similes help convey
> information in *My Brother Martin*, "Hopes and Dreams of Young People,"
> and "When You Hope, Wish, and Trust." Reread all three passages and list
> all the similes and metaphors and their meanings. Then write one paragraph
> in which you introduce the topic, develop the topic with definitions and
> examples from all three texts, and use linking words to connect information.

_____

_____

_____

_____

_____

_____

_____

_____

_____

_____

_____

_____

_____

_____

_____

_____

_____

Connect the Texts
Informative/Explanatory Summary

Student Prompt, p. 168 Summarize the way metaphors and similes help convey information in *My Brother Martin*, "Hopes and Dreams of Young People," and "When You Hope, Wish, and Trust." Reread all three passages and list all the similes and metaphors and their meanings. Then write one paragraph in which you introduce the topic, develop the topic with definitions and examples from all three texts, and use linking words to connect information.

Writing to Sources Define similes and metaphors for students. Have them review the texts to find examples of both types of figurative language. Then have students prepare one-paragraph summaries of how the various writers use similes and metaphors. Remind them to clearly introduce the topic, develop it with definitions and examples, and link their ideas with words.

			Informative/Explanatory Writing Rubric		
Score	**Focus**	**Organization**	**Development of Evidence**	**Language and Vocabulary**	**Conventions**
4	Main idea is clearly conveyed and well supported; response is focused.	Organization is clear and effective, creating a sense of cohesion.	Evidence is relevant and thorough; includes facts and details.	Ideas are clearly and effectively conveyed, using precise language and/or domain-specific vocabulary.	Command of conventions is strongly demonstrated.
3	Main idea is clear, adequately supported; response is generally focused.	Organization is clear, though minor flaws may be present and some ideas may be disconnected.	Evidence is adequate and includes facts and details.	Ideas are adequately conveyed, using both precise and more general language; may include domain-specific vocabulary.	Command of conventions is sufficiently demonstrated.
2	Main idea is somewhat supported; lacks focus or includes unnecessary material.	Organization is inconsistent, and flaws are apparent.	Evidence is uneven or incomplete; insufficient use of facts and details.	Ideas are unevenly conveyed, using overly-simplistic language; lacks domain-specific vocabulary.	Command of conventions is uneven.
1	Response may be confusing, unfocused; main idea insufficiently supported.	Organization is poor or nonexistent.	Evidence is poor or nonexistent.	Ideas are conveyed in a vague, unclear, or confusing manner.	There is very little command of conventions.
0	The response shows no evidence of the ability to construct a coherent explanatory essay using information from sources.				

© Common Core State Standards

Writing 2. Write informative/explanatory texts to examine a topic and convey ideas and information clearly. **Writing 9.** Draw evidence from literary or informational texts to support analysis, reflection, and research. **Writing 9.a.** Apply grade 4 Reading standards to literature (e.g., Describe in depth a character, setting, or event in a story or drama, drawing on specific details in the text [e.g., a character's thoughts, words, or actions].").
Writing 9.b. Apply grade 4 Reading standards to informational texts (e.g., "Explain how an author uses reasons and evidence to support particular points in a text").

Write Like a Reporter
Informative/Explanatory Paragraph

Student Prompt Reread *Jim Thorpe's Bright Path,* and then summarize the impact of Thorpe's family on his athletic career. In a single paragraph, introduce the topic clearly. Give facts and examples from the text that show the influence of Thorpe's brother, mother, and father on his life in sports. Use phrases such as *because of, in reaction to,* and *inspired by* to link your ideas.

_____

_____

_____

_____

_____

_____

_____

_____

_____

_____

_____

_____

_____

_____

_____

_____

Write Like a Reporter

Informative/Explanatory Paragraph

> **Student Prompt, p. 170** Reread *Jim Thorpe's Bright Path,* and then summarize the impact of Thorpe's family on his athletic career. In a single paragraph, introduce the topic clearly. Give facts and examples from the text that show the influence of Thorpe's brother, mother, and father on his life in sports. Use phrases such as *because of, in reaction to,* and *inspired by* to link your ideas.

Writing to Sources After students reread the biography, discuss how Jim Thorpe related to his brother, his mother, and his father. Have students list at least one key thing Thorpe learned from each family member. Then have students write a paragraph to summarize the influence that Thorpe's family had on him. Remind them to clearly introduce the topic, give information using examples and facts, and connect ideas with phrases.

Students' paragraphs should:

- introduce the topic clearly
- develop the topic with facts and examples
- link ideas within and across categories of information using phrases
- demonstrate strong command of the conventions of standard written English

© **Common Core State Standards**

Writing 2. Write informative/explanatory texts to examine a topic and convey ideas and information clearly. **Writing 9.** Draw evidence from literary or informational texts to support analysis, reflection, and research. **Writing 9.b.** Apply grade 4 Reading standards to informational texts (e.g., "Explain how an author uses reasons and evidence to support particular points in a text").

Connect the Texts
Informative/Explanatory Summary

Student Prompt Using details from *Jim Thorpe's Bright Path* and "Special Olympics, Spectacular Athletes," summarize how sports can contribute to a person's well being. Carefully reread both selections. Make notes about the benefits of sports experiences. Then write one paragraph in which you clearly state your topic and develop it with concrete details and examples. Use precise language to make your summary informative.

_____

_____

_____

_____

_____

_____

_____

_____

_____

_____

_____

_____

_____

_____

Connect the Texts
Informative/Explanatory Summary

Student Prompt, p. 172 Using details from *Jim Thorpe's Bright Path* and "Special Olympics, Spectacular Athletes," summarize how sports can contribute to a person's well being. Carefully reread both selections. Make notes about the benefits of sports experiences. Then write one paragraph in which you clearly state your topic and develop it with concrete details and examples. Use precise language to make your summary informative.

Writing to Sources Have students reread *Jim Thorpe's Bright Path* and list the benefits Thorpe got from his sports experiences. Then have students list similar benefits from "Special Olympics, Spectacular Athletes." Tell students to use concrete details and examples from both texts to write a one-paragraph summary of the benefits of sports experiences. Remind students to use precise language as they develop their summaries.

Informative/Explanatory Writing Rubric					
Score	Focus	Organization	Development of Evidence	Language and Vocabulary	Conventions
4	Main idea is clearly conveyed and well supported; response is focused.	Organization is clear and effective, creating a sense of cohesion.	Evidence is relevant and thorough; includes facts and details.	Ideas are clearly and effectively conveyed, using precise language and/or domain-specific vocabulary.	Command of conventions is strongly demonstrated.
3	Main idea is clear, adequately supported; response is generally focused.	Organization is clear, though minor flaws may be present and some ideas may be disconnected.	Evidence is adequate and includes facts and details.	Ideas are adequately conveyed, using both precise and more general language; may include domain-specific vocabulary.	Command of conventions is sufficiently demonstrated.
2	Main idea is somewhat supported; lacks focus or includes unnecessary material.	Organization is inconsistent, and flaws are apparent.	Evidence is uneven or incomplete; insufficient use of facts and details.	Ideas are unevenly conveyed, using overly-simplistic language; lacks domain-specific vocabulary.	Command of conventions is uneven.
1	Response may be confusing, unfocused; main idea insufficiently supported.	Organization is poor or nonexistent.	Evidence is poor or nonexistent.	Ideas are conveyed in a vague, unclear, or confusing manner.	There is very little command of conventions.
0	The response shows no evidence of the ability to construct a coherent explanatory essay using information from sources.				

Ⓒ Common Core State Standards

Writing 2. Write informative/explanatory texts to examine a topic and convey ideas and information clearly. **Writing 9.** Draw evidence from literary or informational texts to support analysis, reflection, and research. **Writing 9.b.** Apply grade 4 Reading standards to informational texts (e.g., "Explain how an author uses reasons and evidence to support particular points in a text").

Write Like a Reporter
Informative/Explanatory Paragraph

Student Prompt Reread *How Tía Lola Came to Stay* with the purpose of summarizing how Tía Lola and the boys change the colonel's hard heart. List the main events. Then begin your one-paragraph summary by stating your topic. Develop the topic with facts and quotations. Use vocabulary from the story to help explain how Tía Lola and the baseball team help the colonel change.

_____

_____

_____

_____

_____

_____

_____

_____

_____

_____

_____

_____

_____

Write Like a Reporter

Informative/Explanatory Paragraph

Student Prompt, p. 174 Reread *How Tía Lola Came to Stay* with the purpose of summarizing how Tía Lola and the boys change the colonel's hard heart. List the main events. Then begin your one-paragraph summary by stating your topic. Develop the topic with facts and quotations. Use vocabulary from the story to help explain how Tía Lola and the baseball team help the colonel change.

Writing to Sources As students reread the story, have them list each event that relates to the colonel in chronological order. Before they begin their paragraphs, point out that, even though the idea to "change a hard heart" is expressed on p. 400, Tía Lola might have been working on the project before then. Remind students to clearly state the topic, use facts and quotations to develop their topic, and use vocabulary from the story to help make their points.

Students' paragraphs should:

- introduce the topic clearly
- develop the topic with facts and quotations
- use domain-specific vocabulary to convey information
- demonstrate strong command of the conventions of standard written English

---

© Common Core State Standards

Writing 2. Write informative/explanatory texts to examine a topic and convey ideas and information clearly. **Writing 9.** Draw evidence from literary or informational texts to support analysis, reflection, and research. **Writing 9.a.** Apply grade 4 Reading standards to literature (e.g., "Describe in depth a character, setting, or event in a story or drama, drawing on specific details in the text [e.g., a character's thoughts, words, or actions].").

Connect the Texts
Informative/Explanatory Summary

Student Prompt Reread the story and the autobiography "The Difficult Art of Hitting" and summarize the feelings that Miguel and Sadaharu Oh share about playing baseball. Use concrete details and quotations from both texts to express how each ballplayer feels about the sport. In one paragraph, give a general observation about them, and then focus on the role baseball plays in their lives. Link ideas about their feelings with words and phrases such as *similar, alike, share,* and *in common.*

_____

_____

_____

_____

_____

_____

_____

_____

_____

_____

_____

_____

_____

_____

_____

_____

Connect the Texts
Informative/Explanatory Summary

Student Prompt, p. 176 Reread the story and the autobiography "The Difficult Art of Hitting" and summarize the feelings that Miguel and Sadaharu Oh share about playing baseball. Use concrete details and quotations from both texts to express how each ballplayer feels about the sport. In one paragraph, give a general observation about them, and then focus on the role baseball plays in their lives. Link ideas about their feelings with words and phrases such as *similar, alike, share,* and *in common.*

Writing to Sources Discuss how readers know that baseball means a lot to Miguel and Sadaharu Oh. As they reread the texts, make sure students note feelings the two have in common. Guide them to select illustrative details and quotations. Remind students to begin their paragraphs with a general observation and then focus on specific details. Encourage them to use a variety of linking words to clarify their information.

Informative/Explanatory Writing Rubric				
Score	Focus	Organization	Development of Evidence	Language and Vocabulary	Conventions
4	Main idea is clearly conveyed and well supported; response is focused.	Organization is clear and effective, creating a sense of cohesion.	Evidence is relevant and thorough; includes facts and details.	Ideas are clearly and effectively conveyed, using precise language and/or domain-specific vocabulary.	Command of conventions is strongly demonstrated.
3	Main idea is clear, adequately supported; response is generally focused.	Organization is clear, though minor flaws may be present and some ideas may be disconnected.	Evidence is adequate and includes facts and details.	Ideas are adequately conveyed, using both precise and more general language; may include domain-specific vocabulary.	Command of conventions is sufficiently demonstrated.
2	Main idea is somewhat supported; lacks focus or includes unnecessary material.	Organization is inconsistent, and flaws are apparent.	Evidence is uneven or incomplete; insufficient use of facts and details.	Ideas are unevenly conveyed, using overly-simplistic language; lacks domain-specific vocabulary.	Command of conventions is uneven.
1	Response may be confusing, unfocused; main idea insufficiently supported.	Organization is poor or nonexistent.	Evidence is poor or nonexistent.	Ideas are conveyed in a vague, unclear, or confusing manner.	There is very little command of conventions.
0	The response shows no evidence of the ability to construct a coherent explanatory essay using information from sources.				

© Common Core State Standards

Writing 2. Write informative/explanatory texts to examine a topic and convey ideas and information clearly. **Writing 9.** Draw evidence from literary or informational texts to support analysis, reflection, and research. **Writing 9.a.** Apply grade 4 Reading standards to literature (e.g., "Describe in depth a character, setting, or event in a story or drama, drawing on specific details in the text [e.g., a character's thoughts, words, or actions]."). **Writing 9.b.** Apply grade 4 Reading standards to informational texts (e.g., "Explain how an author uses reasons and evidence to support particular points in a text").

Write Like a Reporter
Informative/Explanatory Paragraph

Student Prompt Reread *A Gift from the Heart,* and then summarize Little One's reasons for sacrificing her doll. Before you begin, think about the setting and characters in the play. Then, in one paragraph, clearly introduce the topic and develop it with facts, concrete details, and quotations from the drama. Use any special vocabulary you need to help inform about the topic.

_____

_____

_____

_____

_____

_____

_____

_____

_____

_____

_____

_____

_____

_____

_____

_____

Write Like a Reporter
Informative/Explanatory Paragraph

Student Prompt, p. 178 Reread *A Gift from the Heart,* and then summarize Little One's reasons for sacrificing her doll. Before you begin, think about the setting and characters in the play. Then, in one paragraph, clearly introduce the topic and develop it with facts, concrete details, and quotations from the drama. Use any special vocabulary you need to help inform about the topic.

Writing to Sources After students reread the drama, discuss Little One's motivations. Encourage students to talk about the context in which she lives and makes her decision. Tell them to look at the play and find facts, concrete details, and quotations that illustrate her reasons for sacrificing the doll. Then guide students to clearly introduce the topic of motivation in their paragraphs. Remind them to use evidence from the text and domain-specific vocabulary to inform their readers.

Students' paragraphs should:

- introduce the topic clearly
- develop the topic with facts, concrete details, and quotations
- use domain-specific vocabulary to convey information about the topic
- demonstrate strong command of the conventions of standard written English

---

© Common Core State Standards

Writing 2. Write informative/explanatory texts to examine a topic and convey ideas and information clearly. **Writing 9.** Draw evidence from literary or informational texts to support analysis, reflection, and research. **Writing 9.a.** Apply grade 4 Reading standards to literature (e.g., "Describe in depth a character, setting, or event in a story or drama, drawing on specific details in the text [e.g., a character's thoughts, words, or actions].").

Connect the Texts
Informative/Explanatory Summary

Student Prompt Review "Vote for Bluebonnet Day" and the end of *A Gift from the Heart* to summarize what the bluebonnet means to people. Begin your paragraph with a general observation based on both texts. Then focus on what the flower symbolizes. Use quotations and examples from both texts. Connect ideas from the texts using linking phrases such as *in addition* and *in the same way*.

_____

_____

_____

_____

_____

_____

_____

_____

_____

_____

_____

_____

_____

_____

_____

_____

Connect the Texts
Informative/Explanatory Summary

Student Prompt, p. 180 Review "Vote for Bluebonnet Day" and the end of *A Gift from the Heart* to summarize what the bluebonnet means to people. Begin your paragraph with a general observation based on both texts. Then focus on what the flower symbolizes. Use quotations and examples from both texts. Connect ideas from the texts using linking phrases such as *in addition* and *in the same way.*

Writing to Sources Ask students to describe the bluebonnet flower. Explain that they will write one paragraph, based on the texts, that summarizes the flower's symbolism. They must use quotations and examples from both texts to infer the meaning. Guide them to use phrases to link the evidence from the texts that supports their inferences.

			Informative/Explanatory Writing Rubric		
Score	**Focus**	**Organization**	**Development of Evidence**	**Language and Vocabulary**	**Conventions**
4	Main idea is clearly conveyed and well supported; response is focused.	Organization is clear and effective, creating a sense of cohesion.	Evidence is relevant and thorough; includes facts and details.	Ideas are clearly and effectively conveyed, using precise language and/or domain-specific vocabulary.	Command of conventions is strongly demonstrated.
3	Main idea is clear, adequately supported; response is generally focused.	Organization is clear, though minor flaws may be present and some ideas may be disconnected.	Evidence is adequate and includes facts and details.	Ideas are adequately conveyed, using both precise and more general language; may include domain-specific vocabulary.	Command of conventions is sufficiently demonstrated.
2	Main idea is somewhat supported; lacks focus or includes unnecessary material.	Organization is inconsistent, and flaws are apparent.	Evidence is uneven or incomplete; insufficient use of facts and details.	Ideas are unevenly conveyed, using overly-simplistic language; lacks domain-specific vocabulary.	Command of conventions is uneven.
1	Response may be confusing, unfocused; main idea insufficiently supported.	Organization is poor or nonexistent.	Evidence is poor or nonexistent.	Ideas are conveyed in a vague, unclear, or confusing manner.	There is very little command of conventions.
0	The response shows no evidence of the ability to construct a coherent explanatory essay using information from sources.				

ⓒ Common Core State Standards

Writing 2. Write informative/explanatory texts to examine a topic and convey ideas and information clearly. **Writing 9.** Draw evidence from literary or informational texts to support analysis, reflection, and research. **Writing 9.a.** Apply grade 4 Reading standards to literature (e.g., "Describe in depth a character, setting, or event in a story or drama, drawing on specific details in the text [e.g., a character's thoughts, words, or actions]."). **Writing 9.b.** Apply grade 4 Reading standards to informational texts (e.g., "Explain how an author uses reasons and evidence to support particular points in a text").

Write Like a Reporter
Informative/Explanatory Paragraph

Student Prompt Reread *The Man Who Went to the Far Side of the Moon* to prepare a one-paragraph summary of the setting in which Michael Collins spent his time in space. Focus either on the setting inside or outside the spacecraft. Make a list of facts and concrete details to use in your summary. Then write one paragraph, beginning with a general observation. Use vocabulary from the text to describe the setting.

_____

_____

_____

_____

_____

_____

_____

_____

_____

_____

_____

_____

_____

_____

Write Like a Reporter
Informative/Explanatory Paragraph

> **Student Prompt, p. 182** Reread *The Man Who Went to the Far Side of the Moon* to prepare a one-paragraph summary of the setting in which Michael Collins spent his time in space. Focus either on the setting inside or outside the spacecraft. Make a list of facts and concrete details to use in your summary. Then write one paragraph, beginning with a general observation. Use vocabulary from the text to describe the setting.

Writing to Sources Remind students that a setting includes place and time. Have them reread *The Man Who Went to the Far Side of the Moon* to list facts and concrete details about the interior or exterior setting of Michael Collins's space flight. Explain that their paragraphs should begin with a general observation, which might be about the duration of the flight or its purpose. They should follow this with a focused description using evidence and vocabulary from the text.

Students' paragraphs should:
- provide a general observation and then focus on the interior or exterior setting
- develop a summary using facts and concrete details
- use vocabulary from the text to explain the setting
- demonstrate strong command of the conventions of standard written English

Ⓒ **Common Core State Standards**

Writing 2. Write informative/explanatory texts to examine a topic and convey ideas and information clearly. **Writing 9.** Draw evidence from literary or informational texts to support analysis, reflection, and research. **Writing 9.b.** Apply grade 4 Reading standards to informational texts (e.g., "Explain how an author uses reasons and evidence to support particular points in a text").

Connect the Texts
Informative/Explanatory Paragraph

Student Prompt Explain how you would use the online directory from "195 Days in Space" to learn more about *The Man Who Went to the Far Side of the Moon*. From the expository text, select two or three quotations and examples you could investigate further on the Web. Choose two or three new links you could follow. Write one paragraph in which you clearly introduce the topic and connect information from the two readings. Use phrases such as *in order to* and *as result of* to organize your paragraph.

_____

_____

_____

_____

_____

_____

_____

_____

_____

_____

_____

_____

_____

Connect the Texts
Informative/Explanatory Paragraph

Student Prompt, p. 184 Explain how you would use the online directory from "195 Days in Space" to learn more about *The Man Who Went to the Far Side of the Moon.* From the expository text, select two or three quotations and examples you could investigate further on the Web. Choose two or three new links you could follow. Write one paragraph in which you clearly introduce the topic and connect information from the two readings. Use phrases such as *in order to* and *as result of* to organize your paragraph.

Writing to Sources Ask students to explain how they would conduct Internet research about the 1969 trip to the moon. Then have them explain their plan in a paragraph that uses details from both readings. After they list the quotations, examples, and links from the texts, guide them to introduce their topic clearly and link ideas using phrases.

Informative/Explanatory Writing Rubric				
Score	Focus	Organization	Development of Evidence	Language and Vocabulary	Conventions
4	Main idea is clearly conveyed and well supported; response is focused.	Organization is clear and effective, creating a sense of cohesion.	Evidence is relevant and thorough; includes facts and details.	Ideas are clearly and effectively conveyed, using precise language and/or domain-specific vocabulary.	Command of conventions is strongly demonstrated.
3	Main idea is clear, adequately supported; response is generally focused.	Organization is clear, though minor flaws may be present and some ideas may be disconnected.	Evidence is adequate and includes facts and details.	Ideas are adequately conveyed, using both precise and more general language; may include domain-specific vocabulary.	Command of conventions is sufficiently demonstrated.
2	Main idea is somewhat supported; lacks focus or includes unnecessary material.	Organization is inconsistent, and flaws are apparent.	Evidence is uneven or incomplete; insufficient use of facts and details.	Ideas are unevenly conveyed, using overly-simplistic language; lacks domain-specific vocabulary.	Command of conventions is uneven.
1	Response may be confusing, unfocused; main idea insufficiently supported.	Organization is poor or nonexistent.	Evidence is poor or nonexistent.	Ideas are conveyed in a vague, unclear, or confusing manner.	There is very little command of conventions.
0	The response shows no evidence of the ability to construct a coherent explanatory essay using information from sources.				

© Common Core State Standards

Writing 2. Write informative/explanatory texts to examine a topic and convey ideas and information clearly. **Writing 9.** Draw evidence from literary or informational texts to support analysis, reflection, and research. **Writing 9.b.** Apply grade 4 Reading standards to informational texts (e.g., "Explain how an author uses reasons and evidence to support particular points in a text").

Prove It!
Cause-Effect Essay

Influencing Achievement

Informative/Explanatory Cause-Effect Essay

In this unit, students have read examples of cause-effect essays and have had the opportunity to write in this mode. Remind students of texts and writing tasks (such as Write Like a Reporter and Connect the Texts) in which they have encountered and practiced informative/explanatory writing.

Key Features of an Informative/Explanatory Cause-Effect Essay

- identifies the event or condition that produces a certain result—the cause
- explains the outcome or result—the effect
- supports the relationship between causes and effects using examples, facts, details, and quotations
- uses signal words to link ideas and show relationships
- is organized logically to make the explanation clear
- uses precise language and domain-specific vocabulary
- includes an introduction and a conclusion

Writing Task Overview

Each unit writing task provides students with an opportunity to write to sources. To successfully complete the task, students must analyze, synthesize, and evaluate multiple complex texts and create their own written response.

Influencing Achievement

Part 1: Students will reread and take notes on the selected sources. They will then respond to several questions about these sources and discuss their written responses with partners or in small groups.

Part 2: Students will work individually to plan, write, and revise their own informative/explanatory cause-effect essay.

Scorable Products: evidence-based short responses, informative/explanatory cause-effect essay

Influencing Achievement: Writing Task – Short Response

Teacher Directions:

1. **Introduce the Sources** Refer students to the following texts in the Student Edition:

   1. *My Brother Martin,* pp. 328–341

   2. *Jim Thorpe's Bright Path,* pp. 356–371

   3. *How Tía Lola Came to Stay,* pp. 388–403

   Explain to students that they will need to draw evidence and support from the texts above in order to answer evidence-based short response questions and to write a cause-effect essay. Students should take notes and categorize information as they closely reread the texts. Students should be given paper or a relevant graphic organizer from the TR DVD for note-taking.

2. **Provide Student Directions and Scoring Information (p. 190)** Answer any task-related questions students may have. If necessary, provide additional paper for students to write their responses.

3. **Initiate the Writing Task** If you are timing this part of the task, you may wish to alert students when half the allotted time has elapsed and again when 5 minutes remain.

4. **Facilitate Collaboration** After students have completed their written responses to the evidence-based short response questions, assign partners or small groups and have them discuss their responses. If students struggle to work together productively, provide them with tips and strategies for expressing their ideas and building on the ideas of others.

ⓒ Common Core State Standards

Writing 2. Write informative/explanatory texts to examine a topic and convey ideas and information clearly. **Speaking/Listening 1.** Engage effectively in a range of collaborative discussions (one-on-one, in groups, and teacher-led) with diverse partners on grade 4 topics and texts, building on others' ideas and expressing their own clearly. **(Also Writing 2.a., Writing 2.b., Writing 2.c., Writing 2.d.)**

Scoring Information

Use the following 2-point scoring rubrics to evaluate students' answers to the evidence-based short response questions.

1. Compare how Martin, Jim, and Tía Lola change throughout the texts. Include details and examples from the texts as support.

Analysis Rubric	
2	The response: • demonstrates the ability to analyze similarities and differences among the texts • includes specific details that make reference to the texts
1	The response: • demonstrates a limited ability to analyze similarities and differences among the texts • includes some details that make reference to the texts
0	A response receives no credit if it demonstrates no ability to analyze similarities and differences among the texts or includes no relevant details from the texts.

2. Compare how the actions or words of others caused a change in the views, attitudes, or goals of Martin, Jim, and the Colonel. Include specific details and quotations from the texts.

Synthesis Rubric	
2	The response: • demonstrates the ability to synthesize causes and effects among the texts • includes specific details that make reference to the texts
1	The response: • demonstrates a limited ability to synthesize causes and effects among the texts • includes some details that make reference to the texts
0	A response receives no credit if it demonstrates no ability to synthesize information from the sources or includes no relevant details from the texts.

3. Based on the texts, what most influences the way people think and act? Make a judgment and cite details and examples from the texts to support your answer.

Evaluation Rubric	
2	The response: • demonstrates the ability to evaluate causes and effects among the texts • includes specific details that make reference to the texts
1	The response: • demonstrates a limited ability to evaluate causes and effects among the texts • includes some details that make reference to the texts
0	A response receives no credit if it demonstrates no ability to evaluate information from the sources or includes no relevant details from the texts.

Influencing Achievement
Writing Task – Short Response

Student Directions:

Your Assignment You will reread several selections from Unit 6 and take notes on these sources. Then you will answer three questions about these materials. You may refer to your notes or to any of the sources as often as you like.

Sources

1. *My Brother Martin,* pp. 328–341

2. *Jim Thorpe's Bright Path,* pp. 356–371

3. *How Tía Lola Came to Stay,* pp. 388–403

Be sure to read closely and take good notes. Your sources and notes will be the basis for writing your own cause-effect essay in the second half of the writing task.

Evidence-Based Short Response Questions Answer the short response questions on the lines provided below each question. Your answers to these questions will be scored. Be sure to base your answers on the sources you have just read. Remember that you may refer back to your notes or to any of the sources.

After you have answered the questions, you will discuss your responses with a partner or within a small group. Your teacher will let you know when to begin the discussion part of this task.

Scoring Information Your responses will be scored based on how you demonstrate the ability to:

- compare information across texts
- include specific details that highlight relationships between events
- identify, analyze, synthesize, and evaluate information from the texts
- include only relevant details and ideas from sources as support

Evidence-Based Short Response Questions

1. Compare how Martin, Jim, and Tía Lola change throughout the texts. Include details and examples from the texts as support.

_____

_____

_____

_____

2. Compare how the actions or words of others caused a change in the views, attitudes, or goals of Martin, Jim, and the Colonel. Include specific details and quotations from the texts.

_____

_____

_____

_____

3. Based on the texts, what most influences the way people think and act? Make a judgment and cite details and examples from the texts to support your answer.

_____

_____

_____

_____

Collaborative Discussion

After you have written your responses to the questions, discuss your ideas. Your teacher will assign you a partner or a small group and let you know when to begin.

Influencing Achievement: Writing Task – Cause-Effect Essay

Teacher Directions:

1. **Provide Student Directions and Scoring Information (p. 194)** Explain to students that they will now review their notes and sources, and plan, draft, and revise their essays. Although they may use their notes and sources, they must work alone. Students will be allowed to look back at the answers they wrote to the short response questions, but they are not allowed to make changes to those answers. Have students read the directions for the cause-effect essay and answer any task-related questions they may have. Students should be given paper on which to write their essays.

2. **Initiate the Writing Task** If you are timing this part of the task, you may wish to suggest approximate times for students to begin writing and revising. If students wish to continue writing rather than revising, allow them to do so. Alert students when 5 minutes remain.

3. **Scoring Information** Use the scoring rubric on the next page to evaluate students' cause-effect essays.

4. **Cause-Effect Essay Prompt** Use what you have learned from reading *My Brother Martin, Jim Thorpe's Bright Path,* and *How Tía Lola Came to Stay* to write a cause-effect essay about how our abilities, combined with others' views of the world, can influence our dreams and goals. Use examples from the selections to support your ideas. Be sure to follow the conventions of written English.

4-Point Informative/Explanatory Writing Rubric					
Score	Focus	Organization	Development of Evidence	Language and Vocabulary	Conventions
4	Main idea is clearly conveyed and well supported; essay is focused.	Organization is clear and effective, creating a sense of cohesion.	Evidence is relative and thorough; includes facts and details.	Ideas are clearly and effectively conveyed, using precise language and/or domain-specific vocabulary.	Command of conventions is strongly demonstrated.
3	Main idea is clear and adequately supported; essay is generally focused.	Organization is clear, though minor flaws may be present, and some ideas may be disconnected.	Evidence is adequate and includes facts and details.	Ideas are adequately conveyed, using both precise and more general language; may include domain-specific vocabulary.	Command of conventions is sufficiently demonstrated.
2	Main idea is somewhat supported; lacks focus or includes unnecessary material.	Organization is inconsistent, and flaws are apparent.	Evidence is uneven or incomplete; insufficient use of facts or details.	Ideas are unevenly conveyed, using simplistic language; lacks domain-specific vocabulary.	Command of conventions is uneven.
1	Essay may be confusing or unfocused; main idea insufficiently supported.	Organization is poor or nonexistent.	Evidence is poor or nonexistent.	Ideas are conveyed in a vague, unclear, or confusing manner.	There is very little command of conventions.
0	The response shows no evidence of the ability to construct a coherent cause-effect essay using information from sources.				

Ⓒ Common Core State Standards

Writing 2. Write informative/explanatory texts to examine a topic and convey ideas and information clearly. **Writing 9.** Draw evidence from literary or informational texts to support analysis, reflection, and research. **(Also Writing 2.a., Writing 2.b., Writing 2.d., Writing 10.)**

Influencing Achievement
Writing Task – Cause-Effect Essay

Student Directions:

Your Assignment Now you will review your notes and sources, and plan, draft, and revise your cause-effect essay. While you may use your notes and refer to the sources, you must work on your own. You may also refer to the answers you wrote to earlier questions, but you cannot change those answers.

Cause-Effect Essay Prompt Use what you have learned from reading *My Brother Martin, Jim Thorpe's Bright Path,* and *How Tía Lola Came to Stay* to write a cause-effect essay about how our abilities, combined with others' views of the world, can influence our dreams and goals. Use examples from the selections to support your ideas. Be sure to follow the conventions of written English.

Scoring Information Your cause-effect essay will be assigned a score for

1. **Focus** – how well you keep your focus and express your views clearly
2. **Organization** – how logically you present and link ideas and successfully use transitions
3. **Elaboration** – how thoroughly you develop your ideas and support them with facts, definitions, details, quotations, or other information from the texts
4. **Language and Vocabulary** – how effectively you use precise language and domain-specific vocabulary to convey ideas
5. **Conventions** – how well you apply the conventions of grammar, usage, punctuation, capitalization, and spelling

Now begin work on your cause-effect essay. Try to manage your time carefully so that you can

- plan your cause-effect essay
- write your cause-effect essay
- revise and edit for a final draft

Influencing Achievement: Writing Task – Cause-Effect Essay

Teacher Directions:

1. Publish Explain to students that publishing their writing is the last step in the writing process. If time permits, have students review one another's compositions and incorporate any comments their classmates have. Discuss different ways technology can be used to publish writing.

2. Present Students will now have the option to present their cause-effect essays. Have them give speeches on their essays in front of the class. Use the list below to offer students some tips on listening and speaking.

While Listening to a Classmate...
- Give the speaker your full attention.
- Face the speaker and listen carefully.
- Watch for facial expressions, tone of voice changes, and gestures that the speaker may use to explain key ideas.
- Record what the speaker says.

While Speaking to Classmates...
- Make eye contact with your listeners.
- Use good posture, and speak as clearly as you can.
- Use gestures or change your tone of voice to emphasize important ideas.

Things to Do Together...
- Ask and answer questions to clarify ideas and details.
- Build on the ideas of your classmates.

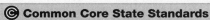 **Common Core State Standards**

Writing 6. With some guidance and support from adults, use technology, including the Internet, to produce and publish writing as well as to interact and collaborate with others; demonstrate sufficient command of keyboarding skills to type a minimum of one page in a single sitting. **Speaking/Listening 1.b.** Follow agreed-upon rules for discussions and carry out assigned roles. **Speaking/Listening 1.c.** Pose and respond to specific questions to clarify or follow up on information, and make comments that contribute to the discussion and link to the remarks of others. **Speaking/Listening 4.** Report on a topic or text, tell a story, or recount an experience in an organized manner, using appropriate facts and relevant, descriptive details to support main ideas or themes; speak clearly at an understandable pace.

More Connect the Texts

More Connect the Texts
Persuasive Essay

STEP 1 Read Like a Writer

Review the key features of a persuasive essay listed below. Respond to any questions students might have.

Key Features of a Persuasive Essay

- Uses a topic sentence to state the writer's opinion, or claim
- Supports the claim with reasons that include facts, details, and examples
- Uses persuasive words to make reasons more convincing
- Provides a conclusion that restates the opinion
- Tries to convince readers to think or act in a certain way

Choose a persuasive text that students have already read to model key features. Display the model for students to see and point out each of the key features you have discussed.

STEP 2 Organize Your Ideas

Writing Prompt Look back at *Because of Winn-Dixie* and *Letters Home from Yosemite.* Think about the personality descriptions of Miss Franny and John Muir that are given or implied in the text. Then make a case as to whether or not Miss Franny and John Muir might have been friends had they met. Support your opinions with details from the texts.

Think Aloud You learned a lot about Miss Franny in *Because of Winn-Dixie,* but you'll need to decide what John Muir was like from information in *Letters from Yosemite.* Decide on the opinion, or claim, you will state in your essay. Then decide which facts, details, and examples you will draw from each selection to support your opinion.

Guided Writing Display an outline as an example. Help students organize reasons that support their opinion, or claim, into the outline. Tell students to write their main idea as a topic sentence and then write a paragraph for each reason. Each paragraph will include facts, details, and examples that support the topic sentence.

STEP 3 Draft Your Writing

Have students use their outlines to write a persuasive essay. Remind them of the key features of a persuasive essay.

Think Aloud An effective way to persuade readers is to support your opinion with details and examples of the characters' traits. Gather details and examples from *Because of Winn-Dixie* and *Letters Home from Yosemite* and also infer John Muir's character traits. You can find additional facts and details about John Muir in books and on Web sites.

Getting Started Tell students to begin writing their persuasive essay using their outlines as a guide. Help them understand where to place facts and supporting details. Emphasize the importance of using correct grammar and clear and coherent writing. Remind them to restate their opinion in their conclusion.

STEP 4 Evaluate Your Writing

Display the checklist below and have students use it to evaluate their persuasive essays. Circulate around the room and confer with individual students.

- ✓ Did I clearly state my position in the topic sentence?
- ✓ Did I include convincing facts, details, and examples that help persuade my readers?
- ✓ Did I organize my reasons in a clear and logical order?
- ✓ Did I use words that appeal to the reader's emotions?
- ✓ Did I conclude by restating my opinion or position?

Help students set goals and a plan for improving in areas where their writing needs to be better.

STEP 5 Revise and Publish

Help students follow through with their plans for revision. If time permits, have students trade essays and offer up suggestions for how to improve their writing.

Publishing Students can print and compile their persuasive essays in a book for classmates to read and comment.

More Connect the Texts
Movie Review

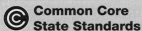
STEP 1 Read Like a Writer

Review the key features of a movie review listed below. Respond to any questions students might have.

Key Features of a Movie Review

- Grabs the reader's attention with something intriguing about the movie
- Uses a topic sentence to state the writer's opinion, or claim
- Supports the opinion with reasons that include facts and details
- Provides a conclusion that restates the opinion
- Uses language that influences what readers will think or do

Choose a movie review to model key features. Display the model for students to see and point out each of the key features you have discussed.

STEP 2 Organize Your Ideas

Writing Prompt Some of Laura Ingalls Wilder's stories have been made into television movies. Suppose *On the Banks of Plum Creek* is a made-for-TV movie. If Opal Buloni were to see the movie, do you think she would or would not like it? Write a review of *On the Banks of Plum Creek* from Opal's point of view. Draw your conclusions based on what you know about Opal from reading *Because of Winn Dixie.* Use evidence from the texts to support your claim.

Think Aloud Your review will be more effective if you think about what Opal thinks and feels before you start writing. Then decide on the opinion that you will state in your movie review. Use facts, supporting details, and examples from the texts to support your claim.

Guided Writing Display a T-chart as an example. Have students create a topic sentence that states Opal's opinion and write the sentence at the top of the chart. Then tell students to jot down reasons for their opinion on one side of the chart. On the other side, students list facts, details, and examples from both texts that support the claim. Then have students use the charts to write Opal's movie review.

STEP 3 Draft Your Writing

Have students use their T-charts to write Opal's review of the movie. Remind them of the key features of a movie review.

Think Aloud When writing your movie review, provide a summary of the plot but don't give away all the information. You don't want your readers to know everything about the movie. Remember that you are writing the review as if you were Opal.

Getting Started Tell students to begin writing their movie review using their T-charts as a guide. Help them decide where to use facts and details. Emphasize the importance of using persuasive words in order to convince the reader of the claim. Remind students to provide a concluding statement.

STEP 4 Evaluate Your Writing

Display the checklist below and have students use it to evaluate their movie reviews. Circulate around the room and confer with individual students.

✓ Did I clearly state the opinion in the topic sentence?

✓ Did I include facts, details, and examples that help support the opinion?

✓ Did I organize my writing in a clear and logical order?

✓ Did I use persuasive words that convince readers to think like I do?

✓ Did I conclude by restating my opinion or position?

✓ Did I check for correct spelling, grammar, and punctuation?

Help students set goals and make a plan for improving in areas where their writing needs to be better.

STEP 5 Revise and Publish

Help students follow through with their plans for revision. If time permits, have students trade movie reviews and offer suggestions for adding relevant evidence.

Publishing Students may e-mail their movie reviews to family and friends.

More Connect the Texts
Persuasive Essay

STEP 1 Read Like a Writer

Review the key features of a persuasive essay listed below. Respond to any questions students might have.

Key Features of a Persuasive Essay
- Establishes a clear position, or claim, on an issue or question
- Supports the claim with reasons that include pertinent facts and examples
- Uses persuasive words to make reasons more convincing
- Tries to convince readers to think or act in a certain way
- Organizes reasons in a clear and logical order

Choose a persuasive essay that students have already read to model key features. Display the model for students to see and point out each of the key features you have discussed.

STEP 2 Organize Your Ideas

Writing Prompt Look back at *Cliff Hanger* and *Antarctic Journal: Four Months at the Bottom of the World.* Both texts discuss risky decisions people make. Write a persuasive essay in which you convince readers that taking risks can be a good thing. Use facts and details from the texts to support the opinion presented.

Think Aloud Your ideas will be more convincing if they are well organized and presented in a logical order. Decide what facts and details you will draw from *Cliff Hanger* and *Antarctic Journal: Four Months at the Bottom of the World* to support your opinion.

Guided Writing Help students organize the ideas that support their opinion into an outline. Explain to them that they will write a paragraph for each idea, with the main point conveyed in the topic sentence. Each paragraph will include facts and details that support the topic sentence.

STEP 3 Draft Your Writing

Have students use their outlines to write a persuasive essay. Remind them of the key features of a persuasive essay.

Think Aloud One of the best ways to persuade readers that your opinion is correct is to use facts and details that support your opinion. Gather facts and details from *Cliff Hanger* and *Antarctic Journal: Four Months at the Bottom of the World*. You can also use your own experiences to provide additional facts and details.

Getting Started Tell students to begin writing their persuasive essay by using their outlines to keep on track. Give students suggestions on where to place their facts and supporting details. Emphasize the importance of using correct grammar and complete sentences. Remind students to end with a concluding statement related to the opinion presented.

STEP 4 Evaluate Your Writing

Display the checklist below and have students use it to evaluate their persuasive essays. Circulate around the room and confer with individual students.

   ✓ Is my position supported by enough details, reasons, facts, and examples?
   ✓ Is my claim, or point of view, stated clearly in the introduction of the essay?
   ✓ Are my supporting details organized into paragraphs in the body?
   ✓ Are my opinion and reasons linked with words and phrases?
   ✓ Does my persuasive essay end with a concluding statement?

Help students set goals and make a plan for improving in areas where their writing needs to be better.

STEP 5 Revise and Publish

Help students follow through with their plans for revision. If time permits, have students trade persuasive essays and offer suggestions for how to improve their writing.

Publishing Students can set up a class blog and post their persuasive essays for friends and family members to read and comment.

More Connect the Texts
Advertising Brochure

Objectives

- Identify the characteristics of an advertising brochure.
- Write an advertising brochure using facts and supporting details.
- Evaluate your writing.
- Revise and publish your writing.

© Common Core State Standards

Writing 1. Write opinion pieces on topics or texts, supporting a point of view with reasons and information. **Writing 4.** Produce clear and coherent writing in which the development and organization are appropriate to task, purpose, and audience. **Writing 5.** With guidance and support from peers and adults, develop and strengthen writing as needed by planning, revising, and editing. **Writing 6.** With some guidance and support from adults, use technology, including the Internet, to produce and publish writing as well as to interact and collaborate with others; demonstrate sufficient command of keyboarding skills to type a minimum of one page in a single setting. **Writing 8.** Recall relevant information from experiences or gather relevant information from print and digital sources; take notes and categorize information, and provide a list of sources. **Writing 9.** Draw evidence from literary or informational texts to support analysis, reflection, and research. **Writing 10.** Write routinely over extended time frames (time for research, reflection, and revision) and shorter time frames (a single setting or a day or two) for a range of discipline-specific tasks, purposes, and audiences.

STEP 1 Read Like a Writer

Review the key features of an advertising brochure listed below. Respond to any questions students might have.

Key Features of an Advertising Brochure

- Organizes information simply, clearly, and succinctly
- Uses bulleted points or small paragraphs for easy reading
- Includes pictures, charts, or illustrations to explain or organize information
- Appeals to the reader
- Has a concluding statement

Choose an advertising brochure that students have already read to model key features. Display the model for students to see and point out each of the key features you have discussed.

STEP 2 Organize Your Ideas

Writing Prompt Look back at "Riding the Rails to Machu Picchu" and "A Walk on the Moon." Both texts discuss trips—but very different ones. Think about how both of these trips might appeal to people. Then write an advertising brochure showcasing both trips, convincing readers to go on either of the two trips. Use facts and details from the texts to support the opinions presented.

Think Aloud Your ideas will be more convincing if they draw the reader in. Decide which interesting facts and details you will pull from "Riding the Rails to Machu Picchu" and "A Walk on the Moon" to support your opinions.

Guided Writing Display an outline as an example. Help students organize the ideas that support their opinion into an outline. Explain to them that they will write either short paragraphs or bulleted lists to support their ideas.

STEP 3 Draft Your Writing

Have students use their outlines to write the advertising brochure. Remind them of the key features of an advertising brochure.

Think Aloud One of the best ways to persuade readers is to use language that attracts them. Use appealing adjectives and verbs when presenting the facts and details you gathered from "Riding the Rails to Machu Picchu" and "A Walk on the Moon."

Getting Started Tell students to begin writing their advertising brochures by using their outlines to keep them organized. Give them suggestions about where they might use short paragraphs and where they might use bulleted lists in the brochure. Emphasize the importance of using correct grammar and complete sentences. Remind students to end with a concluding statement related to the opinion presented.

STEP 4 Evaluate Your Writing

Display the checklist below and have students use it to evaluate their advertising brochures. Circulate around the room and confer with individual students.

- ✓ Did I state my information simply, clearly, and succinctly?
- ✓ Did I present my text in short paragraphs or as bulleted points?
- ✓ Did I include pictures, charts, or illustrations to help explain or organize the information?
- ✓ Did I use language that appeals to the reader?
- ✓ Did I provide a concluding statement?

Help students set goals and make a plan for improving in areas where their writing needs to be better.

STEP 5 Revise and Publish

Help students follow through with their plans for revision. If time permits, have students trade advertising brochures and offer up suggestions for how to improve their writing.

Publishing Students can set up a class Web site and post their advertising brochures for friends and family members to read and comment.

More Connect the Texts
Book Review

Objectives

- Identify the characteristics of a book review.
- Write a book review using facts and supporting details.
- Evaluate your writing.
- Revise and publish your writing.

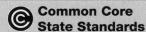

Common Core State Standards

Writing 1. Write opinion pieces on topics or texts, supporting a point of view with reasons and information. **Writing 4.** Produce clear and coherent writing in which the development and organization are appropriate to task, purpose, and audience. **Writing 5.** With guidance and support from peers and adults, develop and strengthen writing as needed by planning, revising, and editing. **Writing 6.** With some guidance and support from adults, use technology, including the Internet, to produce and publish writing as well as to interact and collaborate with others; demonstrate sufficient command of keyboarding skills to type a minimum of one page in a single sitting. **Writing 9.** Draw evidence from literary or informational texts to support analysis, reflection, and research.

Step 1 Read Like a Writer

Review the key features of a book review that are listed below. Respond to any questions students might have.

Key Features of a Book Review

- Begins with the title and author of the book
- Tells what the book is about
- Discusses the book's theme or message
- Gives an opinion about the book and supports it with facts and details
- Provides a concluding statement related to the opinion

Discuss book reviews that students may have written in the past and the key features of a book review. If a model is available, display it for students and point out each of the key features you have discussed.

Step 2 Organize Your Ideas

Writing Prompt Look back at *Coyote School News* and think about the part horses play in Monchi's life. What do you think Monchi would have thought about *Horse Heroes: True Stories of Amazing Horses*? Write a book review of *Horse Heroes* from Monchi's point of view. Use details from both texts to support your opinions about the book.

Think Aloud Before you begin writing, use details from *Coyote School News* to get a sense of Monchi's character and how he feels about horses. Then make sure you write the way you think he would sound. Include the main ideas you think would be important to Monchi and his opinion of the book based on his experience. Use facts, details, and examples to support the opinion.

Guided Writing Have students outline the parts of the story they will include in their book review. They will write a paragraph for each idea, using a topic sentence with supporting details. Remind students that their book reviews will consist of an overview and not everything that happens in the story. Their conclusion should include Monchi's opinion along with reasons.

Step 3 Draft Your Writing

Have students use their outlines to write a book review from Monchi's point of view. Remind students of the key features of a book review.

Think Aloud Your book review should give your readers enough information to decide whether or not they want to read the book. State the main points of the book clearly and provide support with details and examples. You might want to include a quotation from the book.

Getting Started Tell students to begin writing their book reviews using their outlines to keep them on track. Encourage them to determine if they have chosen the best parts of the story to write about. Students can revise their outlines if they wish. Emphasize the importance of precise language and using different sentence structures. Remind them to state their opinion in their conclusion.

Step 4 Evaluate Your Writing

Display the checklist below and have students use it to evaluate their book reviews. Circulate around the room and confer with individual students.

- ✓ Did I include the title and author of the book in the first paragraph?
- ✓ Did I include a topic sentence with supporting details in each paragraph?
- ✓ Did I organize my book review in a logical way?
- ✓ Did I use correct capitalization?
- ✓ Did I discuss the theme of the book?
- ✓ Did I give an opinion of the book?

Help students set goals and develop a plan for improving in areas where their writing needs further development.

Step 5 Revise and Publish

Help students follow through with their plans for revision. If time permits, have students trade book reviews and offer up suggestions for how to improve their writing.

Publishing Students can set up a class blog and post their book reviews for friends and family members to read and comment.

More Connect the Texts
Persuasive Speech

Step 1 Read Like a Writer

Review the key features of a persuasive speech listed below. Respond to any questions students might have.

Key Features of a Persuasive Speech

- Attempts to get support for an idea or claim
- States the claim in a topic sentence
- Supports the claim with facts, details, and examples
- Uses persuasive words to try to convince readers
- Concludes by restating the claim

Choose a persuasive speech to read to students to model key features or the writing form. Display the model for students to see and point out each of the key features you have discussed.

Step 2 Organize Your Ideas

Writing Prompt Reread pp. 212–213 in *Coyote School News* and the poem "Home" on p. 252 and think about why home and family are special. Then write a persuasive speech entitled "There's No Place Like Home." Use examples and details from both texts to develop your speech.

Think Aloud Your ideas will be more convincing and have more impact if they are presented in a logical, precise way. Think about the meaning of "There's No Place Like Home." Then think about what details and examples you will draw from *Coyote School News* and "Home" to support that claim.

Guided Writing Display a T-chart with the titles of the texts as heads. Have students list reasons or examples of why home and family are important under the corresponding heading. Then have students choose the most important items and decide the order in which to write about them. Remind students that each paragraph should have a main idea and supporting details.

Step 3 Draft Your Writing

Have students use their T-charts to write a persuasive speech. Remind them of the key features of a persuasive speech.

Think Aloud Remember to use persuasive words and examples and details that support your ideas. You want your readers to agree with you that home and family are very important.

Getting Started Tell students to begin writing their persuasive speeches using their T-charts to guide them. Guide them in deciding where to place facts and supporting details that will help persuade their audience. Make suggestions of how to link opinion and reasons using persuasive words and convincing phrases. Emphasize the importance of using correct spelling and punctuation. Remind students to restate their positions or opinions in their conclusion.

Step 4 Evaluate Your Writing

Display the checklist below and have students use it to evaluate their persuasive speeches. Circulate around the room and confer with individual students.

- ✓ Did I establish the claim at the beginning of my speech?
- ✓ Did I focus on one main idea and include supporting details in each paragraph?
- ✓ Did I organize my speech in a logical way?
- ✓ Did I use correct spelling and punctuation?
- ✓ Did I use persuasive words in my speech?
- ✓ Did I conclude by restating my claim?

Help students set goals and develop a plan for improving in areas where their writing needs to be strengthened.

Step 5 Revise and Publish

Help students follow through with their plans for revision. If time permits, have students trade speeches and offer up suggestions for how to improve their writing.

Publishing Students can share and discuss their completed speeches with the rest of the class or with family members.

More Connect the Texts
Business Proposal

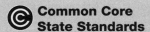

Objectives

- Identify the characteristics of a business proposal.
- Write a business proposal using facts and supporting details.
- Evaluate your writing.
- Revise and publish your writing.

Ⓒ Common Core State Standards

Writing 1. Write opinion pieces on topics or texts, supporting a point of view with reasons and information. **Writing 4.** Produce clear and coherent writing in which the development and organization are appropriate to task, purpose, and audience. **Writing 5.** With guidance and support from peers and adults, develop and strengthen writing as needed by planning, revising, and editing. **Writing 9.** Draw evidence from literary or informational texts to support analysis, reflection, and research.

Step 1 Read Like a Writer

Review the key features of a business proposal listed below. Respond to any questions students might have.

Key Features of a Business Proposal

- States the writer's idea or suggestion
- Tells why the idea is a good one and why the writer should be involved
- Tries to influence the reader's opinion by giving strong reasons for the proposal
- Supports the reasons with facts, details, and examples
- Restates the idea or suggestion in the closing paragraph

Display a business proposal as a model for students. Point out each of the key features.

Step 2 Organize Your Ideas

Writing Prompt Look back at *What Jo Did* and *Scene Two.* Jo has strong athletic skills and Angie is a leader and works well with people. Imagine the girls want to start a sports/drama summer camp at the local park district. Write a proposal from the point of view of both girls briefly describing the program and why they are the ideal individuals to run the program. Support your claims by citing evidence from each text.

Think Aloud Jo and Angie know that they are the best-qualified people to run the camp. Jo is good at basketball, and Angie works well with people. Write Jo's and Angie's qualifications on two character webs. Then decide some details or examples you might add to make them appealing to people reading the proposal.

Guided Writing Display an outline on which to organize ideas. Help students write a strong opinion sentence. Suggest that they include the athletic and organizational abilities of both girls in one paragraph and their people skills in another. Remind students that each paragraph begins with a topic sentence and is supported with facts, examples, and details.

Step 3 Draft Your Writing

Have students use their outlines to write their proposals. Remind them of the key features of a business proposal

Think Aloud Remember that Jo and Angie need to sell themselves in their proposal. Use a positive tone so readers can "hear" how confident they sound. You want your readers to understand what an asset the two girls would be. Provide examples of accomplishments that will make them stand out.

Getting Started Tell students to use their outlines to begin writing their proposals. Provide guidance as to which facts, details, and examples will have the most impact on readers. Remind students to restate their claims in their closing paragraph.

Step 4 Evaluate Your Writing

Display the checklist below and have students use it to evaluate their proposals. Circulate around the room and confer with individual students.

- ✓ Did I state my position clearly in a topic sentence?
- ✓ Did I provide strong reasons why Jo and Angie are the best individuals to run the camp?
- ✓ Did I organize my essay in a logical way?
- ✓ Did I use a variety of interesting verbs?
- ✓ Do Jo's and Angie's personalities shine through?
- ✓ Did I conclude by restating my position?

Help students set goals and a plan for improving in areas where their writing needs to be strengthened.

Step 5 Revise and Publish

Help students follow through with their plans for revision. If time permits, have students trade proposals and offer suggestions for how to improve their writing.

Publishing Students can submit their proposals to an adult to critique.

More Connect the Texts
Persuasive Advertisement

Step 1 Read Like a Writer

Review the key features of a persuasive advertisement listed below. Respond to any questions students might have.

Key Features of a Persuasive Advertisement

- Grabs reader's attention
- States a claim about a product, a service, or an idea
- Uses details to urge readers to take action or make a purchase
- Uses convincing language
- Provides a concluding statement related to the claim

Choose an advertisement from a print or online source to model key features. Display the model for students to see and point out each of the key features you have discussed.

Step 2 Organize Your Ideas

Writing Prompt: Imagine that Encyclopedia Brown and Drake and Nell from *The Case of the Gasping Garbage* decide to open a detective school together. Write a persuasive advertisement in which you convince readers to enroll in the school. Use details from the each text to persuade readers and support your opinion.

Think Aloud Your ideas will be more convincing if they get the reader interested in what you are promoting. Decide which interesting details you will draw from *The Case of the Gasping Garbage* and *Encyclopedia Brown* to support your opinion.

Guided Writing Display an outline as an example. Have students organize their ideas in an outline by helping them decide what their main reasons for enrolling in the school will be. Then have them list details below these ideas.

Step 3 Draft Your Writing

Have students use their outlines to write a persuasive advertisement. Remind them of the key features of a persuasive advertisement.

Think Aloud Think about what you might say that would get readers interested in the detective school, supporting your reasons with details from *The Case of the Gasping Garbage* and *Encyclopedia Brown.* Use appealing adjectives and strong verbs throughout the advertisement to convince readers.

Getting Started Tell students to begin writing their persuasive advertisements by using their outlines to keep them organized. Give them suggestions about what kinds of attention-grabbing opening statements they might use to draw readers in and keep them reading. Emphasize the importance of using correct grammar and complete sentences. Remind students to end with a concluding statement related to the claim presented.

Step 4 Evaluate Your Writing

Display the checklist below and have students use it to evaluate their persuasive advertisements. Circulate around the room and confer with individual students.

✓ Did I include an attention-grabbing introductory statement?
✓ Did I take a position about my idea?
✓ Did I use details to urge readers to take action?
✓ Did I use language that persuades the reader?
✓ Did I provide a concluding statement?

Help students set goals and develop a plan for improving in areas where their writing needs to be strengthened.

Step 5 Revise and Publish

Help students follow through with their plans for revision. If time permits, have students trade persuasive advertisements and offer up suggestions for how to improve their writing.

Publishing Students can email their persuasive advertisements to friends and family members.

More Connect the Texts
Persuasive Speech

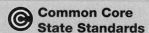
Step 1   Read Like a Writer

Review the key features of a persuasive speech listed below. Respond to any questions students might have.

Key Features of a Persuasive Speech

- Clearly states an opinion at the beginning
- Supports the opinion with facts, details, and explanations
- Uses convincing language
- Provides a concluding statement related to the opinion

Display a model of a persuasive speech for students to see and point out each of the key features you have discussed.

Step 2   Organize Your Ideas

Writing Prompt "Making Mummies" and "The Young Detectives of Potterville Middle School" both discuss what we can learn about past events and people through research and investigation. Write a persuasive speech asking Potterville Middle School to allow their students to examine mummies in their lab. Use details from the texts to support the opinion presented.

Think Aloud Think about what the students in "The Young Detectives of Potterville Middle School" learn in their lab at school. Then think about what we know about mummies, as discussed in "Making Mummies." Decide what useful information the students could learn by studying mummies.

Guided Writing Display an outline as an example. Have students organize their ideas in an outline by helping them decide what the main reasons for studying mummies would be. Then have them list details below these ideas, using information in the texts as a reference.

Step 3 Draft Your Writing

Have students use their outlines to write a persuasive speech. Remind them of the key features of a persuasive speech.

Think Aloud Remember to use effective language to help you emphasize your argument and support each point with details.

Getting Started Tell students to begin writing their persuasive speeches by using their outlines to keep them organized. Help them list their points in a logical order. Emphasize the importance of using correct grammar and complete sentences. Remind students to end with a concluding statement related to the opinion presented.

Step 4 Evaluate Your Writing

Display the checklist below and have students use it to evaluate their persuasive speeches. Circulate around the room and confer with individual students.

- ✓ Did I clearly state a claim at the beginning?
- ✓ Did I support the claim with facts, details, and explanations?
- ✓ Did I use language that persuades the reader?
- ✓ Did I provide a concluding statement?

Help students set goals and develop a plan for improving in areas where their writing needs to be strengthened.

Step 5 Revise and Publish

Help students follow through with their plans for revision. If time permits, have students trade persuasive speeches and offer suggestions for how to improve their writing.

Publishing Students can print and then present their speeches to the class.

More Connect the Texts
Letter of Recommendation

Step 1 Read Like a Writer

Review the key features of a letter of recommendation listed below. Respond to any questions students might have.

Key Features of a Letter of Recommendation

- Includes a date and a salutation, or greeting
- Includes an introduction that describes the purpose of the letter
- Has a body that consists of several paragraphs
- Provides a concluding statement related to the opinion

Display a model of a letter of recommendation for students to see and point out each of the key features you have discussed.

Step 2 Organize Your Ideas

Writing Prompt Look back at *Seeker of Knowledge* and *Encyclopedia Brown.* Both texts discuss solving mysteries. Write a letter of recommendation telling why Jean-François Champollion and Encyclopedia Brown should be honored with an award for their mystery-solving abilities. Use facts and concrete details from the texts to support your key ideas.

Think Aloud Think about the mysteries that Jean-François Champollion and Encyclopedia Brown solved. Then decide what was most important about them.

Guided Writing Display an outline as an example. Have students organize their ideas in an outline by having them list the main reasons for recommending Champollion and Encyclopedia Brown. Then have them list details below these ideas, using information from the texts as a reference.

Step 3 Draft Your Writing

Have students use their outlines to write their letters. Remind them of the key features of a letter of recommendation.

Think Aloud Decide on the structure of your letter. Choose whether you will discuss Champollion or Encyclopedia Brown first. Then use appropriate details from the texts to support your points.

Getting Started Tell students to begin writing their letters by using their outlines to keep them organized. Remind them to use effective language that stresses why Champollion and Encyclopedia Brown should be given an award for their work. Emphasize the importance of using correct grammar and complete sentences. Have students end with a concluding statement related to the opinion presented.

Step 4 Evaluate Your Writing

Display the checklist below and have students use it to evaluate their letters. Circulate around the room and confer with individual students.

✓ Did I include a date and a salutation?
✓ Did I include an introduction that tells why I am writing the letter?
✓ Did I include several paragraphs in the body of the letter?
✓ Did I provide a concluding statement?

Help students set goals and a plan for improving in areas where their writing needs to be better.

Step 5 Revise and Publish

Help students follow through with their plans for revision. If time permits, have students trade their letters of recommendation and offer suggestions for how to improve their writing.

Publishing Students can set up a class blog and post their letters of recommendation for friends and family members to read.

Nomination Letter

Step 1 Read Like a Writer

Review the key features of a nomination letter listed below. Respond to any questions students might have.

Key Features of a Nomination Letter

- States the writer's opinion, or claim
- Includes a heading, address, salutation, body, closing, and signature
- Tries to influence the reader's opinion with strong reasons
- Supports the reasons with facts, details, and examples
- Restates the claim in the closing paragraph

Display a nomination letter as a model. Have students read and point out each of the key features you have discussed.

Step 2 Organize Your Ideas

Writing Prompt Look back at *The Man Who Named the Clouds* and *Eye of the Storm.* Both texts feature experts. Write a letter nominating Luke Howard and Warren Faidley for "Experts You Should Know." Use evidence from each text to support your arguments.

Think Aloud Your ideas will be more convincing if you choose strong reasons and present them in a logical order. State your opinion, or why you wish to nominate each person, in your letter. Use facts, details, and examples from *The Man Who Named the Clouds* and *Eye of the Storm* to support your opinion. You may wish to use a T-chart to organize the ideas for the body of your letter.

Guided Writing Remind students where to place each part of their letter. Tell them that the first paragraph should state their claim in the topic sentence. The students should organize information about Luke Howard and Warren Faidley in the next two paragraphs. Explain each of those paragraphs will focus on one main idea and will include only the most important facts and details that support the main idea.

Step 3 Draft Your Writing

Have students use their T-charts to write a nomination letter. Remind them of the key features of a nomination letter.

Think Aloud Remember to give strong reasons for your nomination. Use phrases, such as *for instance,* to link your opinion and reasons. You want readers to understand the contributions of each expert. Support your reasons with facts, quotations, and examples from each text.

Getting Started Tell students to use their charts as they begin writing their nomination letters. Provide guidance as to which facts, details, and examples are the strongest. Emphasize using a variety of sentence types and lengths. Remind students to restate their opinion, or claim, in their closing paragraph.

Step 4 Evaluate Your Writing

Display the checklist below and have students use it to evaluate their nomination letter. Circulate around the room and confer with individual students.

- ✓ Did I include all the parts of a letter?
- ✓ Did I state my position clearly in the introduction?
- ✓ Did I provide strong reasons and evidence for why I am nominating each expert?
- ✓ Did I organize my letter in a logical way?
- ✓ Did I conclude by restating my opinion?

Help students set goals and make a plan for improving in areas where their writing needs to be better.

Step 5 Revise and Publish

Help students follow through with their plans for revision. If time permits, have students trade letters and offer suggestions for how to improve their writing.

Publishing Students can e-mail their nomination letters to family and friends.

More Connect the Texts
Persuasive Advertisement

Objectives

- Identify the characteristics of a persuasive advertisement.
- Write a persuasive advertisement using facts and supporting details.
- Evaluate your writing.
- Revise and publish your writing.

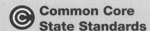

Common Core State Standards

Writing 1. Write opinion pieces on topics or texts, supporting a point of view with reasons and information. **Writing 4.** Produce clear and coherent writing in which the development and organization are appropriate to task, purpose, and audience. **Writing 5.** With guidance and support from peers and adults, develop and strengthen writing as needed by planning, revising, and editing. **Writing 9.** Draw evidence from literary or informational texts to support analysis, reflection, and research.

Step 1 Read Like a Writer

Review the key features of a persuasive advertisement listed below. Respond to any questions students might have.

Key Features of a Persuasive Advertisement

- Contains an opinion, or position, about a product, service, or idea
- Supports the opinion with reasons that include facts, details, and examples
- Organizes reasons in a clear, logical way
- Uses persuasive words to make reasons more convincing
- Restates the opinion in the closing paragraph

Choose a persuasive advertisement to model key features. Display the model for students to read. Help them point out each of the key features you have discussed.

Step 2 Organize Your Ideas

Writing Prompt Look back at pp. 352–354 of *Adelina's Whales* and the selection "A Very Grand Canyon." Each text describes an interesting vacation destination. Write a persuasive essay encouraging readers to visit either Laguna San Ignacio or the Grand Canyon. Support your claim by citing evidence from each text.

Think Aloud I know I have a better chance of persuading readers if I use facts, details, and examples to support my opinion. The first thing I need to do is decide which location I think would be the better vacation destination. I will use a T-chart to help me make that decision. I will list facts, details, and examples from both texts to help me decide which vacation destination I prefer. Then I'll use the appropriate facts to support my claim.

Guided Writing Display a T-chart as an example. Explain that students will write information about Laguna San Ignacio on one side and information about the Grand Canyon on the other. Using that information, students will determine which they think is the better vacation spot and then write their claim with facts and details to support it.

Step 3 Draft Your Writing

Review with students the key features of a persuasive advertisement. Be sure to remind students that they will only use one side of their T-charts when they write their persuasive advertisement.

Think Aloud What did you learn from the texts that would make you want to visit one place more than the other? Give strong reasons that will persuade readers. Support your reasons with facts, quotations, and examples from the text. You may also use books and Web sites to find additional facts and details.

Getting Started Tell students to refer to the appropriate side of their T-charts as they begin writing. Help students determine which of the facts, details, and examples are the strongest and where to place them. Emphasize using colorful adjectives and catchy phrases to make the vacation destination more appealing. Remind students to end with a concluding statement.

Step 4 Evaluate Your Writing

Display the checklist below and have students use it to evaluate their persuasive advertisement. Circulate around the room and confer with individual students.

- ✓ Did I begin with an attention-grabbing statement?
- ✓ Did I state my position clearly, and does it appeal to readers' emotions?
- ✓ Did I provide supporting reasons and details to influence the audience?
- ✓ Did I organize my advertisement in a logical way?
- ✓ Did I restate my opinion in the conclusion?

Help students set goals and make a plan for improving in areas where their writing needs to be better.

Step 5 Revise and Publish

Help students follow through with their plans for revision. If time permits, have partners trade persuasive advertisements and offer suggestions for how to improve their writing.

Publishing Students can display their persuasive advertisements on a bulletin board for classmates to read.

More Connect the Texts
Letter to the Editor

© Common Core State Standards

Writing 1. Write opinion pieces on topics or texts, supporting a point of view with reasons and information. **Writing 4.** Produce clear and coherent writing in which the development and organization are appropriate to task, purpose, and audience. **Writing 5.** With guidance and support from peers and adults, develop and strengthen writing as needed by planning, revising, and editing. **Writing 8.** Recall relevant information from experiences or gather relevant information from print and digital sources; take notes and categorize information, and provide a list of sources. **Writing 9.** Draw evidence from literary or informational texts to support analysis, reflection, and research.

Step 1 Read Like a Writer

Review the key features of a letter to the editor listed below. Respond to any questions students might have.

Key Features of a Letter to the Editor
- Is sent to the editor of a newspaper or magazine
- Is written in response to a story or article, an event, or an issue
- Usually aims to persuade others by supporting claims with clear reasons and relevant evidence
- Establishes and maintains correct formal letter format
- Provides a concluding statement related to the opinion

Display a letter to the editor to model key features. Have students point out each of the key features you have discussed. Tell students that published letters rarely include the full name or address for privacy reasons.

Step 2 Organize Your Ideas

Writing Prompt Look back at *My Brother Martin* and "Special Olympics, Spectacular Athletes." Imagine that these athletes live in your area and the articles appeared in the local newspaper. Write a letter to the editor expressing why the people in the articles serve as an inspiration to others. Use details from the texts to support the opinion presented.

Think Aloud Decide on the main reasons you think the people are an inspiration. Then choose details from *My Brother Martin* and "Special Olympics, Spectacular Athletes" that you will use to support your reasons.

Guided Writing Have students organize their ideas in an outline by helping them choose what their main reasons for inspiration will be. Have them list facts and details from the texts below their reasons. Then explain that they will write a paragraph for each reason, with the main point conveyed in the topic sentence and facts and details conveyed in the body of the paragraph.

Step 3 Draft Your Writing

Have students use their outlines to write a letter to the editor. Remind them of the key features of a letter to the editor.

Think Aloud Begin your letter with a salutation, or greeting. Then write an introductory paragraph that explains why you are writing the letter.

Getting Started Tell students to use their outlines to keep them organized. Remind them that a letter to the editor should use formal language. Emphasize the importance of using correct grammar and complete sentences, Remind students to end with a concluding statement restating the opinion presented.

Step 4 Evaluate Your Writing

Display the checklist below and have students use it to evaluate their letters to the editor. Circulate around the room and confer with individual students.

- ✓ Did I write a letter in response to something I read?
- ✓ Did I try to persuade others by supporting my claim with reasons and evidence?
- ✓ Did I maintain a formal letter format?
- ✓ Did I provide a concluding statement related to my opinion?

Help students set goals and a plan for improving in areas where their writing needs work.

Step 5 Revise and Publish

Help students follow through with their plans for revision. If time permits, have students trade letters to the editor and offer up suggestions for how to improve their writing.

Publishing Students can compile their letters to the editor in a folder and make them available for the class to review.

More Connect the Texts
Product Advertisement

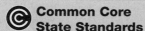
Step 1 Read Like a Writer

Review the key features of a product advertisement listed below. Respond to any questions students might have.

Key Features of a Product Advertisement

- Grabs the reader's attention
- Makes a claim about a product
- Uses catchy words and phrases to urge readers to make a purchase
- Concludes with a restatement of the claim

Choose a product advertisement to model key features. Display the model for students to see and point out each of the key features you have discussed.

Step 2 Organize Your Ideas

Writing Prompt: Look back at *Jim Thorpe's Bright Path* and "The Difficult Art of Hitting." Both texts discuss people who became great athletes. Imagine that Jim Thorpe and Sadaharu Oh created a product together that helps athletes become better at their sport. Write a product advertisement that explains what the product is and how it improves athletes' performance. Use details from the texts to support the opinion presented.

Think Aloud Think about a product that Thorpe and Oh might have used themselves to improve their athletic performance. Give the product a name that will appeal to readers. Then come up with details about the product that you can use in the advertisement.

Guided Writing Have students use note cards to find and write down catchy words and phrases in both texts that could be used to describe the product's effects. For example, your product can help you "push yourself" and "fill your body with fighting spirit."

Step 3 Draft Your Writing

Have students use their note cards to write a product advertisement. Remind them of the key features of a product advertisement.

Think Aloud Think about a way to grab your readers' attention in the advertisement. What can you say to get readers interested in the product?

Getting Started Tell students to refer to their note cards as they begin writing their product advertisements. Remind them that a product advertisement should use persuasive details that get readers to make a purchase.

Step 4 Evaluate Your Writing

Display the checklist below and have students use it to evaluate their product advertisements. Circulate around the room and confer with individual students.

- ✓ Did I grab the reader's attention?
- ✓ Did I state my claim about the product?
- ✓ Did I include details that would encourage readers to buy my product?
- ✓ Did I end by restating my claim?

Help students set goals and develop a plan for improving in areas where their writing needs more work.

Step 5 Revise and Publish

Help students follow through with their plans for revision. If time permits, have students trade product advertisements and offer suggestions for how to improve their writing.

Publishing Students can print their advertisements and then present them to the class as television advertisements.

More Connect the Texts
Application Essay

 Common Core State Standards

Writing 1. Write opinion pieces on topics or texts, supporting a point of view with reasons and information. **Writing 4.** Produce clear and coherent writing in which the development and organization are appropriate to task, purpose, and audience. **Writing 5.** With guidance and support from peers and adults, develop and strengthen writing as needed by planning, revising, and editing. **Writing 6.** With some guidance and support from adults, use technology, including the Internet, to produce and publish writing as well as to interact and collaborate with others; demonstrate sufficient command of keyboarding skills to type a minimum of one page in a single setting. **Writing 9.** Draw evidence from literary or informational texts to support analysis, reflection, and research.

Step 1 Read Like a Writer

Review the key features of an application essay listed below. Respond to any questions students might have.

Key Features of an Application Essay

- States a claim about being a good candidate
- Uses reasons to support the claim
- Uses persuasive language
- Has a formal style
- Provides a concluding statement related to the claim

Choose an application essay that students have already read to model key features. Display the model for students to see and point out each of the key features you have discussed.

Step 2 Organize Your Ideas

Writing Prompt Look back at "Hopes and Dreams of Young People" and *The Man Who Went to the Far Side of the Moon.* Both texts discuss people realizing their dreams. Write an application essay for space camp from the point of view of one of the writers in "Hopes and Dreams of Young People." Tell why you would like to attend space camp, the reasons you are a good candidate, and why you would be a good astronaut. Use details from both texts to support your argument.

Think Aloud Think about what one of the writers in "Hopes and Dreams of Young People" would say in the essay. Decide on the main reasons for attending space camp, using details from the two texts to support your reasons.

Guided Writing Display an outline as an example. Have students organize their ideas in an outline by helping them list their main reasons for attending space camp. Have them list facts and details from the texts below their reasons. Also have them list why they would be good candidates for space camp and the sources they can use as references in their essays.

Step 3 Draft Your Writing

Have students use their outlines to write an application essay. Remind them of the key features of an application essay.

Think Aloud In your introduction, briefly explain what you are applying for and why you think you are a good candidate. Then, in the body of your essay, give facts and details that support those points. Use language that one of the writers in "Hopes and Dreams of Young People" would use.

Getting Started Tell students to begin writing their application essays by using their outlines to keep them organized. Remind them that an application essay should use formal language and should also be persuasive. Emphasize the importance of using correct grammar and complete sentences, and remind students to end with a concluding statement related to the opinion presented.

Step 4 Evaluate Your Writing

Display the checklist below and have students use it to evaluate their application essays. Circulate around the room and confer with individual students.

✓ Did I state a claim about being a good candidate?

✓ Did I support my claim with reasons?

✓ Did I use persuasive language?

✓ Did I maintain a formal letter format?

✓ Did I provide a concluding statement related to my opinion?

Help students set goals and develop a plan for improving in areas where their writing needs more work.

Step 5 Revise and Publish

Help students follow through with their plans for revision. If time permits, have students trade application essays and offer suggestions for how to improve their writing.

Publishing Students can set up a class blog and post their essays for friends and family members to read.

More Connect the Texts
Compare-and-Contrast Essay

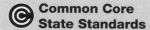

Common Core State Standards

Writing 2. Write informative/explanatory texts to examine a topic and convey ideas and information clearly. **Writing 4.** Produce clear and coherent writing in which the development and organization are appropriate to task, purpose, and audience. **Writing 5.** With guidance and support from peers and adults, develop and strengthen writing as needed by planning, revising, and editing. **Writing 9.** Draw evidence from literary or informational texts to support analysis, reflection, and research.

STEP 1 Read Like a Writer

Review the key features of a compare-and-contrast essay listed below. Respond to any questions students might have.

Key Features of a Compare-and-Contrast Essay

- Compares and contrasts two things by telling how they are alike and different
- Uses transitions and details to show similarities and differences
- States a clear central idea in a topic sentence
- Follows an appropriately organized structure
- Includes supporting sentences with simple facts, details, or explanations

Choose a compare-and-contrast text that students have already read to model key features. Display the model for students to see and point out each of the key features you have discussed.

STEP 2 Organize Your Ideas

Writing Prompt Look back at *Lewis and Clark and Me* and *The Horned Toad Prince*. Compare and contrast the two texts. Consider their organization and graphics as well as their words. Write an explanation of how the texts are alike and how they are different. Provide evidence from the texts to support your ideas.

Think Aloud Your ideas will be more convincing if you organize them in a clear and logical way. Before you begin writing, list the similarities and differences between the two stories on a T-chart. Also, make an outline before you write, showing the order in which you will introduce the similarities and differences.

Guided Writing Display an outline as an example. Help students organize the similarities and differences into an outline. Explain that students will include how the selections are alike in one or two paragraphs and how they are different in other paragraphs. Each paragraph will state the main idea and supporting sentences, which include relevant facts and details from the texts.

STEP 3 Draft Your Writing

Have students use their outlines to write a compare-and-contrast essay. Remind them of the key features of compare and contrast.

Think Aloud Remember that a compare-and-contrast essay tells how two things are alike and different. Explore similarities in one paragraph and differences in another. You can introduce the similarities and differences in any order.

Getting Started Tell students to begin writing their compare-and-contrast essay, using their outlines to help them group related information. Help students understand which facts and supporting details show similarities and which show differences. Remind students to use transition words to link ideas. Emphasize the importance of using correct spelling and punctuation.

STEP 4 Evaluate Your Writing

Display the checklist below and have students use it to evaluate their compare-and-contrast essays. Circulate around the room and confer with individual students.

- ✓ Did I organize similarities in one paragraph and differences in another?
- ✓ Did all of my sentences include concrete details that clearly identify similarities and differences?
- ✓ Did I group similarities and differences in a clear and logical way?
- ✓ Did I use transitions to signal similarities and differences?
- ✓ Did I use a variety of concrete details to support the relationships?
- ✓ Did I summarize the topic in a concluding statement?

Help students set goals and make a plan for improving areas where their writing needs to be better.

STEP 5 Revise and Publish

Help students follow through with their plans for revision. If time permits, have students trade essays so that their peers may offer suggestions for improving their writing.

Publishing Students may trade their completed compare-and-contrast essays with a partner to read and comment.

More Connect the Texts
Compare-and-Contrast Essay

Objectives

- Identify the characteristics of a compare-and-contrast essay.
- Write a compare-and-contrast essay using facts and supporting details.
- Evaluate your writing.
- Revise and publish your writing.

 Common Core State Standards

Writing 2. Write informative/explanatory texts to examine a topic and convey ideas and information clearly. **Writing 4.** Produce clear and coherent writing in which the development and organization are appropriate to task, purpose, and audience. **Writing 5.** With guidance and support from peers and adults, develop and strengthen writing as needed by planning, revising, and editing. **Writing 6.** With some guidance and support from adults, use technology, including the Internet, to produce and publish writing as well as to interact and collaborate with others; demonstrate sufficient command of keyboarding skills to type a minimum of one page in a single sitting. **Writing 8.** Recall relevant information from experiences or gather relevant information from print and digital sources; take notes and categorize information, and provide a list of sources. **Writing 9.** Draw evidence from literary or informational texts to support analysis, reflection, and research. **Writing 10.** Write routinely over extended time frames (time for research, reflection, and revision) and shorter time frames (a single sitting or a day or two) for a range of discipline-specific tasks, purposes, and audiences.

STEP 1 Read Like a Writer

Review the key features of a compare-and-contrast essay listed below. Respond to any questions students might have.

Key Features of a Compare-and-Contrast Essay

- Compares and contrasts two things by telling how they are alike and different
- Uses transitions and details to show similarities and differences
- States a clear central idea in a topic sentence
- Includes supporting sentences with simple facts, details, or explanations
- Follows an appropriately organized structure

Choose a compare-and-contrast essay that students have already read to model key features. Display the model for students to see and point out each of the key features you have discussed.

STEP 2 Organize Your Ideas

Writing Prompt Look back at *Lost City* and "A Walk on the Moon." Both texts discuss exploring new places. Write a compare-and-contrast essay that explains how the explorations described in each text are similar and different. Use facts and concrete details to support your key ideas.

Think Aloud Your ideas will be clearer if you organize them before writing. Decide which similarities and differences you will draw from *Lost City* and "A Walk on the Moon."

Guided Writing Display a Venn diagram as an example. Help students organize their similarities and differences in the diagram. Explain to them that they will write a paragraph for each key idea, with the main point conveyed in the topic sentence. Each paragraph will include facts and concrete details that support the topic sentence.

STEP 3 Draft Your Writing

Have students use their diagrams to write a compare-and-contrast essay. Remind them of the key features of a compare-and-contrast essay.

Think Aloud Decide whether you would like to discuss the similarities or differences first in your essay. Then gather the appropriate facts and concrete details from *Lost City* and "A Walk on the Moon" that you listed in your diagram.

Getting Started Tell students to begin writing their compare-and-contrast essays by using their diagrams to keep them on track. Give them suggestions on where to place their facts and concrete details. Emphasize the importance of using correct grammar and complete sentences. Remind them to end with a concluding statement related to the information presented.

STEP 4 Evaluate Your Writing

Display the checklist below and have students use it to evaluate their compare-and-contrast essays. Circulate around the room and confer with individual students.

- ✓ Did I state the central idea of my compare-and-contrast essay in the introduction?
- ✓ Do all of my sentences tell about similarities and differences?
- ✓ Did I arrange my similarities and differences in a logical order that the audience can follow and understand?
- ✓ Did I use transition words that compare and contrast similarities and differences?
- ✓ Did I end my essay with a concluding statement?

Help students set goals and make a plan for improving in areas where their writing needs to be better.

STEP 5 Revise and Publish

Help students follow through with their plans for revision. If time permits, have students trade compare-and-contrast essays and offer suggestions for how to improve their writing.

Publishing Students can create a multimedia presentation by using props, graphic aids, or computer software to present their essays.

More Connect the Texts
News Article

STEP 1 Read Like a Writer

Review the key features of a news article listed below. Respond to any questions students might have.

Key Features of a News Article

- Reports current events
- Begins with a headline and a byline
- Gives the most important information in the lead
- Includes supporting sentences with facts, details, and explanations
- Often includes text features, such as photos and captions

Choose a news article that students have already read to model key features. Display the model for students to see and point out each of the key features you have discussed.

STEP 2 Organize Your Ideas

Writing Prompt Look back at *Smokejumpers: Life Fighting Fires* and *Antarctic Journal: Four Months at the Bottom of the World.* Both texts discuss real people and adventures. Write a news article about the adventures by using information from the texts. Include facts, concrete details, and quotations to support your key ideas.

Think Aloud Your ideas will be clearer if you organize them before writing. Identify any facts, details, or quotations from *Smokejumpers: Life Fighting Fires* and *Antarctic Journal: Four Months at the Bottom of the World* that you want to include in your article.

Guided Writing Display an outline as an example. Help students organize their ideas in an outline. Explain to them that they will write a paragraph for each key idea, with the main point conveyed in the topic sentence. Each paragraph will include facts, concrete details, and quotations that support the topic sentence.

STEP 3 Draft Your Writing

Have students use their outlines to write a news article. Remind them of the key features of a news article.

Think Aloud A *lead* is the first paragraph of a news article. It contains the topic sentence and some of the important information. Gather together the information you consider most important from *Smokejumpers: Life Fighting Fires* and *Antarctic Journal: Four Months at the Bottom of the World*. Then write the lead using that information.

Getting Started Tell students to begin writing their news articles by using their outlines to keep them on track. Give them suggestions on where to place their facts, concrete details, and quotations. Emphasize the importance of using correct grammar and complete sentences. Remind them to end with a concluding statement related to the information presented.

STEP 4 Evaluate Your Writing

Display the checklist below and have students use it to evaluate their news articles. Circulate around the room and confer with individual students.

  ✓ Did I include a headline and a byline?
  ✓ Did I include the most important information in my lead?
  ✓ Did I include facts, concrete details, and quotations in the body of my article?
  ✓ Did I end my article with a concluding statement?
  ✓ Did I include photos or captions?

Help students set goals and make a plan for improving in areas where their writing needs to be better.

STEP 5 Revise and Publish

Help students follow through with their plans for revision. If time permits, have students trade news articles and offer suggestions for how to improve their writing.

Publishing Students can use computer software to write and design their news articles before presenting them to the class.

More Connect the Texts
How-to Article

Step 1 Read Like a Writer

Review the key features of a how-to article listed below. Respond to any questions students might have.

Key Features of a How-to Article

- Introduces the purpose clearly
- Explains how to do or make something
- Contains a sequence of steps and activities to follow
- Uses time-order transition words
- Provides a conclusion related to the information presented

Show students a how-to article to model key features. Science experiments or cooking recipes are good examples. Display the model and point out each of the key features.

Step 2 Organize Your Ideas

Writing Prompt Reread "How to Start a School Newspaper" on pp. 224–226, paying close attention to the steps in a how-to article. Then reread *Scene Two* on pp. 234–250 and examine the structure of the play. Write a how-to article in which you explain the format for writing a play.

Think Aloud Think about how a play is different from a story. How do you know what the setting is or who is speaking? How do you know what the characters are doing? Make an outline before you start writing.

Guided Writing Display an outline on which students can organize their ideas. Remind students that the first paragraph includes the purpose of their how-to article and the subsequent paragraphs explain how to format a play. Tell students to use words such as *first, next,* and *finally.* Students should include how to indicate stage directions and dialogue.

Step 3 Draft Your Writing

Have students use their outlines to write their how-to articles. Remind them of the key features of how-to articles.

Think Aloud Your ideas will be easier to understand if they are presented in a logical order. You will use your outlines to write the draft of your how-to article. After you have written your how-to-article, follow it to explain how to rewrite the text in a play format.

Getting Started Tell students to begin writing their how-to articles using their outlines as a guide. As they write, suggest that students imagine themselves doing each step. If some steps are not easy to follow, encourage students to add details to make them easier to understand. Students should end with a concluding sentence.

Step 4 Evaluate Your Writing

Display the checklist below and have students use it to evaluate their how-to articles. Circulate around the room and confer with individual students.

- ✓ Did I clearly state my purpose in a topic sentence?
- ✓ Did I include step-by-step instructions?
- ✓ Did I explain the procedure in a logical and precise way?
- ✓ Did I make sure the steps are easy to understand?
- ✓ Did I include a concluding statement that relates to my purpose?

Help students set goals and a plan for improving in areas where their writing needs to be further developed.

Step 5 Revise and Publish

Help students follow through with their plans for revision. If time permits, have students trade articles and offer up suggestions for how to improve their writing.

Publishing Partners can follow the steps in the article to write a play based on a favorite story.

More Connect the Texts
Formal Letter

Objectives

- Identify the characteristics of a formal letter.
- Write a formal letter.
- Evaluate your writing.
- Revise and publish your writing.

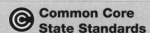 **Common Core State Standards**

Writing 2. Write informative/explanatory texts to examine a topic and convey ideas and information clearly. **Writing 4.** Produce clear and coherent writing in which the development and organization are appropriate to task, purpose, and audience. **Writing 5.** With guidance and support from peers and adults, develop and strengthen writing as needed by planning, revising, and editing. **Writing 9.** Draw evidence from literary or informational texts to support analysis, reflection, and research.

Step 1 Read Like a Writer

Review the key features of a formal letter listed below. Respond to any questions students might have.

Key Features of a Formal Letter

- Includes a heading, address, salutation, body, closing, and signature
- States a clear central idea in a topic sentence
- Includes supporting sentences with facts, details, or explanations
- Focuses on one subject
- Uses a business-like tone

Choose a formal letter to model key features. Display the model for students to see. Point out each of the key features you have discussed.

Step 2 Organize Your Ideas

Writing Prompt Look back at *Coyote School News* and *So You Want to Be President.* Each selection includes information about President Franklin Roosevelt's accomplishments. Write a formal letter to President Roosevelt asking what he believes to be his most meaningful contributions to his country. Use facts and details from each text.

Think Aloud Gather and organize your ideas before you begin writing. You might want to use a word web to cite President Roosevelt's achievements. Include details from the texts. You may wish to use other books or Web sites, too. Find and use a letter template.

Guided Writing Display a template of a formal letter. Help students understand where each component of a formal letter belongs. Explain that a topic sentence in the first paragraph in the body of the letter conveys the reason for writing. The subsequent paragraphs give details and examples that support the topic.

Step 3 Draft Your Writing

Have students use their templates or the model letter to write a formal letter.

Think Aloud Remember that you are writing to a United States president, so you need to use a formal tone. Use a search engine to find the address of the White House. You will use your word webs and letter templates as you write the draft of your letter.

Getting Started Tell students to begin writing their formal letters using their templates if available. Emphasize using correct grammar and clear language. Suggest that students explain at the beginning of their letter that they have read about important things the president did, and they wonder what President Roosevelt views as his most significant accomplishments.

Step 4 Evaluate Your Writing

Display the checklist below and have students use it to evaluate their letters. Circulate around the room and confer with individual students.

- ✓ Did I include all parts of a formal letter?
- ✓ Did I use an appropriate tone in my letter?
- ✓ Did I give a short, simple explanation of why I am writing?
- ✓ Did I focus on my topic and include supporting facts and details?
- ✓ Did I organize the body of my letter in a logical way?

Help students set goals and a plan for improving in areas where their writing needs further development.

Step 5 Revise and Publish

Help students follow through with their plans for revision. If time permits, have students trade letters and offer up suggestions for how to improve their writing.

Publishing Students can trade their completed letters with a partner to read and then reply as if they were President Roosevelt.

More Connect the Texts
Instructions

Step 1 Read Like a Writer

Review the key features of instructions listed below. Respond to any questions students might have.

Key Features of Instructions

- Tell how to do something
- Explain each step in a process
- Often use time-order words, such as *first, next,* and *last*
- Are often written in list form

Use a set of simple instructions to model key features for students. Display the model for students to see and point out each of the key features you have discussed.

Step 2 Organize Your Ideas

Writing Prompt Look back at *Navajo Code Talkers* and *Seeker of Knowledge.* Both texts discuss codes in language and writing. Write instructions for how Jean-François Champollion might have cracked the code of the Navajos, based on how he deciphered Egyptian hieroglyphs. Use facts and concrete details from the texts to support your key ideas.

Think Aloud Your ideas will be clearer if you organize them before writing. Make a list of the steps the Navajos took to create their code. Then make a list of the steps Champollion took to decipher the Egyptian hieroglyphs. Think about how Champollion might have adapted his steps to crack the Navajo's code.

Guided Writing Display a T-chart as an example. Help students organize each of their lists in a column. Remind them that they will apply Champollion's steps to cracking the Navajo code.

Step 3 Draft Your Writing

Have students use their T-charts to write instructions. Remind them of the key features of instructions.

Think Aloud The steps should be listed in a logical order in the instructions. Use appropriate words to indicate the correct order.

Getting Started Tell students to begin writing their instructions by using their T-charts to keep them on track. Have students write a short introductory paragraph that describes what their list is about. Emphasize the importance of using correct grammar and complete sentences.

Step 4 Evaluate Your Writing

Display the checklist below and have students use it to evaluate their instructions. Circulate around the room and confer with individual students.

✓ Did I explain how something is done?
✓ Did I include each step in the process?
✓ Did I use time-order transition words?
✓ Did I write my instructions in list form?

Help students set goals and develop a plan for improving in areas where their writing needs further development.

Step 5 Revise and Publish

Help students follow through with their plans for revision. If time permits, have students trade instructions and offer up suggestions for how to improve their writing.

Publish Students can create a multimedia presentation by using props, graphic aids, or computer software to present their instructions.

More Connect the Texts
Summary

- Identify the characteristics of a summary.
- Write a summary using facts and supporting details.
- Evaluate your writing.
- Revise and publish your writing.

Common Core State Standards

Writing 2. Write informative/explanatory texts to examine a topic and convey ideas and information clearly.
Writing 4. Produce clear and coherent writing in which the development and organization are appropriate to task, purpose, and audience. (Grade-specific expectations for writing types are defined in standards 1–3 above.) **Writing 5.** With guidance and support from peers and adults, develop and strengthen writing as needed by planning, revising, and editing. **Writing 9.** Draw evidence from literary or informational texts to support analysis, reflection, and research.

Step 1 Read Like a Writer

Review the key features of a summary listed below. Respond to any questions students might have.

Key Features of a Summary
- Is a short retelling of a story or an article
- Includes only key events or main ideas
- Retells events in the same sequence as the original story
- Includes only the most important events and details
- Uses the writer's own words

Choose a summary that students have already read to model key features. Display the model for students to see and point out each of the key features you have discussed.

Step 2 Organize Your Ideas

Writing Prompt Myths and tall tales are different types of folklore. *How Night Came From the Sea* is a myth, and *Paul Bunyan* is a tall tale. Reread the section on pp. 442–443 in *Paul Bunyan* that tells how Paul and Babe straighten the Big Onion River. Write a summary of that section in the style of a myth. Remember to include only key events or main ideas, and only important details. Use *How Night Came From the Sea* to help you determine the style to follow.

Think Aloud A myth is an imaginative story that explains something about nature. It builds the plot to a climax and uses details to describe the setting. Think about how you will explain how the Big Onion River got straight. Summarize the event in your own words.

Guided Writing Display an outline on which students can organize their summary. Help students compose a topic sentence. Tell students to include only major events in the summary and to organize them into paragraphs. Guide students in understanding which facts and details are important enough to include.

Step 3 Draft Your Writing

Have students use their outlines to write a summary. Remind them of the key features of a summary.

Think Aloud Your summary will be more effective if you keep the main events in the story in order. You might wish to begin your summary similar to *How Night Came from the Sea* with the words "Long, long ago."

Getting Started Tell students to use their outlines as they begin writing their summaries. Remind them to include only the most important events and details. Emphasize using correct grammar, spelling, and mechanics. Guide students in developing a concluding statement.

Step 4 Evaluate Your Writing

Display the checklist below and have students use it to evaluate their summaries. Circulate around the room and confer with individual students.

✓ Does my opening tell what the summary is about?

✓ Did I include only key events in my summary?

✓ Did I include only important details?

✓ Did I retell the story in the same order as the original?

✓ Did I use my own words?

Help students set goals and make a plan for improving in areas where their writing needs to be better.

Step 5 Revise and Publish

Help students follow through with their plans for revision. If time permits, have students trade summaries and offer up suggestions for how to improve their writing.

Publishing Students can place their summaries in a folder for other students to read.

More Connect the Texts
Expository Composition

Step 1 Read Like a Writer

Review the key features of an expository composition listed below. Respond to any questions students might have.

Key Features of an Expository Composition

- Tells of real people and events and presents factual information
- Includes a topic sentence, a body, and a concluding statement
- May include photos, captions, and subheads

Choose an expository composition that students have already read to model key features. Display the model for students to see and point out each of the key features you have discussed.

Step 2 Organize Your Ideas

Writing Prompt Look back at *My Brother Martin* and *The Man Who Went to the Far Side of the Moon*. Both texts discuss important contributions people have made. Write an expository composition telling how Dr. Martin Luther King Jr. and the astronauts each contributed to society. Use facts and concrete details from the texts to support your key ideas.

Think Aloud Your ideas will be clearer if you organize them before writing. Make a list of the ways King contributed to society. Then make a list of the ways the astronauts contributed to society.

Guided Writing Display a T-chart as an example. Help students organize each of their lists in a column. Have students think about how they will use the lists to write a topic sentence for their composition's introductory paragraph.

Step 3 Draft Your Writing

Have students use their T-charts to write expository compositions. Remind them of the key features of expository compositions.

Think Aloud Decide whether you will discuss King or the astronauts first. Then list each key idea about the men in its own paragraph, along with any related facts and details that support the idea. Separate the sections on King and the astronauts by using subheads.

Getting Started Tell students to begin writing their expository compositions by using their T-charts to keep them on track. Remind students that their introductory paragraph should briefly mention the men's contributions to society. The rest of the composition should then discuss each of those contributions individually. Emphasize the importance of using correct grammar and complete sentences. Remind students to end with a concluding statement.

Step 4 Evaluate Your Writing

Display the checklist below and have students use it to evaluate their instructions. Circulate around the room and confer with individual students.

- ✓ Did I present factual information about real people?
- ✓ Did I include a topic sentence, a body, and a concluding statement?
- ✓ Did I include photos, captions, or subheads?

Help students set goals and develop a plan for improving their writing in areas that need more work.

Step 5 Revise and Publish

Help students follow through with their plans for revision. If time permits, have students trade instructions and offer suggestions for how to improve their writing.

Publishing Students can create a multimedia presentation by using props, graphic aids, or computer software to present their expository compositions.

More Connect the Texts
Summary

Objectives

- Identify the characteristics of a summary.
- Write a summary retelling main ideas and key details.
- Evaluate your writing.
- Revise and publish your writing.

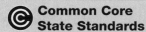

Common Core State Standards

Writing 2. Write informative/explanatory texts to examine a topic and convey ideas and information clearly.
Writing 4. Produce clear and coherent writing in which the development and organization are appropriate to task, purpose, and audience.
Writing 5. With guidance and support from peers and adults, develop and strengthen writing as needed by planning, revising, and editing. **Writing 6.** With some guidance and support from adults, use technology, including the Internet, to produce and publish writing as well as to interact and collaborate with others; demonstrate sufficient command of keyboarding skills to type a minimum of one page in a single setting.
Writing 9. Draw evidence from literary or informational texts to support analysis, reflection, and research.

Step 1 Read Like a Writer

Review the key features of a summary listed below. Respond to any questions students might have.

Key Features of a Summary

- Retells the most important information
- Uses the writer's own words
- Leaves out unimportant details
- Follows a logical order

Choose a summary that students have already read to model key features. Display the model for students to see and point out each of the key features you have discussed.

Step 2 Organize Your Ideas

Writing Prompt Look back at *A Gift From the Heart* and *The Man Who Went to the Far Side of the Moon*. Both texts discuss sacrifices people make on behalf of others. Write a summary of the texts, focusing on the sacrifices Little One and the astronauts make and the benefits of their sacrifices. Use facts and concrete details from the texts to support your key ideas.

Think Aloud Include the most important details from the texts in your summary. Give general information about the events, but place special emphasis on the sacrifices and benefits discussed in each text.

Guided Writing Display an outline as an example. Help students organize the texts' main events in their outlines. Then have them list details under each event.

Step 3 Draft Your Writing

Have students use their outlines to write summaries. Remind them of the key features of summaries.

Think Aloud Write an introductory paragraph that includes information about both texts. Then decide which selection you will discuss first in your summary. Be sure to use your own words when writing your summaries.

Getting Started Tell students to begin writing their summaries by using their outlines to keep them on track. Remind students that their summaries should be much shorter than the texts themselves and should not include unnecessary details. Emphasize the importance of using correct grammar and complete sentences. Remind students to end with a concluding statement.

Step 4 Evaluate Your Writing

Display the checklist below and have students use it to evaluate their summaries. Circulate around the room and confer with individual students.

✓ Did I include only important information in the summary?
✓ Did I write the summary in my own words?
✓ Did I summarize the information in the order of the original texts?
✓ Did I keep my summary short and free of repeated information?
✓ Did I use transition words to help with the flow of the summary?

Help students set goals and develop a plan for improving their writing as needed.

Step 5 Revise and Publish

Help students follow through with their plans for revision. If time permits, have students trade instructions and offer suggestions for how to improve their writing.

Publishing Students can post their summaries on a class Web site and share them with each other.